Flash Books New York London

Clouds Studios/Retna,
Rex Features (inset).
Courtesy of Capitol
Records

George Harrison
Yesterday and Today

by Ross Michaels

George Harrison:
Yesterday and Today

International Standard Book Number:
  0-8256-3913-1
Library of Congress Catalog Card Number:
  77-78536
Printed in the United States of America.

Designed by Jon Goodchild
Discography by Wendy Schacter
Front cover photograph by Michael Zagaris
Back cover photograph by Joseph Sia

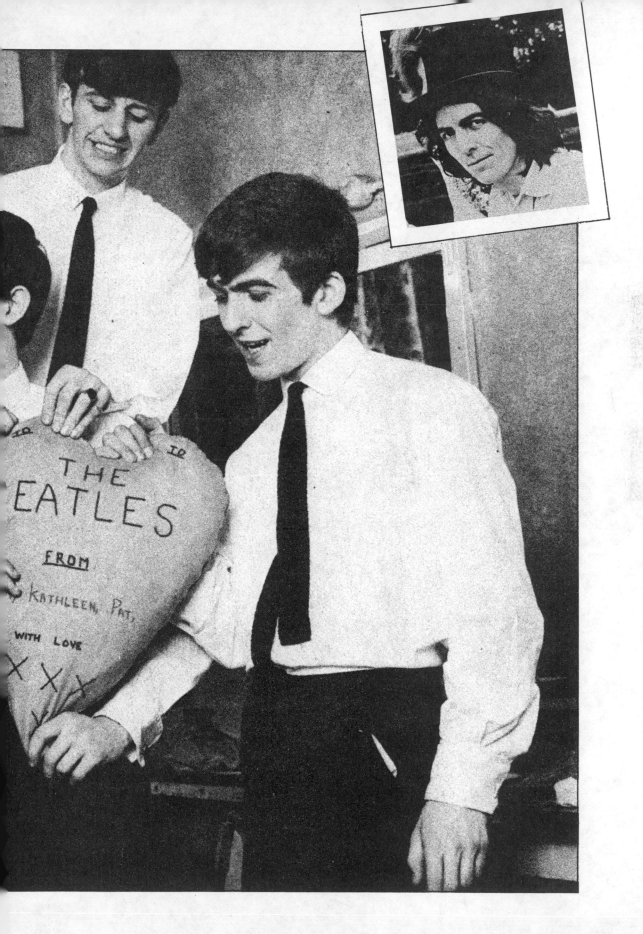

FRIENDS OF US ALL

1 Sunday, August 1, 1971: Stifling heat and humidity in New York. The sky seemed to hang over Manhattan streets like a damp, stinking blanket. A normal weekend afternoon in summer. Masses of New Yorkers had scattered in desperate flight to cooler retreats on farms and beaches, in villages and woods. For the hapless left behind, the city was like it often is on such a day—a victim of sunstroke, floating motionless in its warm grey waters. But this Sunday was going to be different. The patient stirred, or at least a twitch was intensifying near its abdomen.

Thousands of young people were converging on Madison Square Garden in cars, trains, subways, and on foot. A wild current of electricity circuited through everyone drawn toward the massive arena, America's premier rock and roll palace—from the seamy side-streets on the fringe of the garment district in the low 30s between Seventh and Eighth avenues, from underneath the Garden, through the dreary passages of Pennsylvania Station, on to the huge lobby, up the escalators, and into the 20,000-seat hall. They poured in from a hundred ramps and stairways. The Garden buzzed with anticipation, acting on the lethargic city like a concrete-and-glass pancreas secreting waves of adrenalin outward throughout it, preparing it for a dramatic involuntary reaction to a great event.

George Harrison, the Quiet Beatle, the man whose embrace of Eastern philosophy and Krishna consciousness helped catalyze the social revolution in America during the mid-60s, was about to take the stage for a benefit concert to aid the millions of starving, war-weary people of Bangla Desh in their struggle for national survival against East Pakistan. This was Harrison's first full concert appearance in the States since the Beatles' farewell show in August 1966 at Candlestick Park in San Francisco. Harrison's longtime close friend and sitar guru, Ravi Shankar, himself of Bangla Desh, had appealed to Harrison for help in the relief effort. The Concert for Bangla Desh, actually two shows on Sunday, August 1, was Harrison's answer.

A festival euphoria swept through the Garden as the certifiable Cultural Event approached. Rumors, like frisbees and balloons, floated through the haze: Ringo would play drums, and John and Paul would appear onstage for a Beatles reunion. Bob Dylan was seen backstage—no, Dylan was last seen slumped in a limousine inching its way through traffic toward the Garden. Still, this was Harrison's day. The Beatles era had ended when Paul sang *Let It Be* in the spring of 1970, and the post-Beatle era seemed to begin with George's simple but profoundly resonant proclamation, *All Things Must Pass*, in the fall of the same year. That album, among the most accomplished rock LPs of all times, was a stunning personal triumph for Harrison, as it thrust him out of the long and imposing shadows of Lennon and McCartney and into a new life as a solo superstar.

The concert opened with a stirring set of Indian music by a virtual trinity of raga masters—Shankar on sitar; Ali Akbar Khan on the eerie steel-stringed sarod; and Alla Rakha on tabla. During the intermission, house lights and the buzz of expectancy came up. Suddenly the lights came down, a roar went up, and Harrison strode onstage— matured, elegant, and *loose* in a gleaming white suit and orange shirt. His face was neatly framed by thick brown hair and a beard. He promptly opened his set with the low-range, three-note lead-in to his powerful rock cut, "Wah-Wah," from *All Things,* and as his enormous backup band pumped out a 180-degree barrage of support, it was clear the Event would surpass all expectations. The sound was as full and well-orchestrated as any sound on a rock stage could be: there was Ringo Starr on drums; Eric Clapton, the English blues-rock virtuoso, on guitar; Leon Russell, the country-rock legend, on piano; Billy Preston, the exuberantly flashy R & B singer/keyboardist; Jesse Ed Davis, an American Indian, on electric guitar; Jim Horn and his celebrated brass backup section; Jim Keltner, the superb studio drummer from Los Angeles; Klaus Voorman, a Beatle friend from Hamburg, on bass; a female backup vocal group led by the Gospel-strong voice of Claudia Linnear; three acoustic guitar players of the English group Badfinger; and George, slightly hunched over his Fender guitar, cranking his head left and right as he grimaced to reach certain notes.

Harrison dominated the stage with

Opposite:
Joseph Sia.
The Bangladesh
Concert, 1971

Pages 6 and 7:
Rex Features.

9

subtle control and brilliant pacing that led through "My Sweet Lord," "Awaiting on You All," and his chilling "Beware of Darkness," all from his solo LP *All Things Must Pass*. There was Preston's rousing "That's the Way God Planned It," Starr's hit, "It Don't Come Easy," and Russell's raucously funky medley of "Jumpin' Jack Flash/Young Blood." Harrison joined Clapton for a climactic lead guitar dialogue on "While My Guitar Gently Weeps" (Clapton had played on the LP cut, the first non-Beatle to record with them); and Harrison also offered his two most moving Beatle compositions, "Something" and "Here Comes the Sun," featuring his fragile, affecting solo on acoustic guitar.

But the most electrifying moment of the day, when the Event seemed to suddenly transform itself into some kind of *miracle*, was Harrison's colossally understated introduction of "a friend of us all"—Dylan himself, the *other* 60s myth, along with the Beatles. He walked onstage in tan jeans, denim jacket, and a scruffy beard. He looked relaxed, assured, and clutched his guitar across his chest, his harmonica rack crossing his chin. The crowd was stunned, silenced, then erupted in a standing—and for many tearful—roar of affection. Dylan said nothing, but just opened with strumming and the first lines of his classic, "A Hard Rain's Gonna Fall," filled with its urgent apocalyptic imagery from nearly a decade before. His voice wasn't the consciously mannered, hollowed-out croon of *Nashville Skyline* but the pained cathartic wail of his earliest, most inflamed creations. He then kept the promise implied in his first selection and stuck to Dylan gems: "Mr. Tambourine Man," "Blowin' in the Wind," and two others—"It Takes a Lot to Laugh, It Takes a Train to Cry" and "Just Like a Woman." His harmonica glistened and cut through spotlighted shafts of light like a buzzsaw splitting lumber. The set ended—almost a shimmering pop culture mirage—with Harrison playing delicate slide guitar fills, Ringo on tambourine, and Russell on bass, and contributing descending hillbilly-style harmonies to Dylan's repeated phrase "Just like a woman" in the finale.

The 20,000 fans left the Garden after Harrison ended the show with his politically minded hit single, "Bangla Desh." They poured back onto the streets, into subway cars, suburban trains, and cars, creating monumental traffic jams. It didn't matter. They were dazed, muttering, as if drunk with contemplation of what they had witnessed. Two Beatles—Harrison and Starr—Dylan, Clapton, Russell, Shankar. Comparisons to Woodstock were inevitable, but ultimately specious. This was arguably the most formidable assemblage of pop music heroes on any single bill, and it would become the single most successful rock benefit project of its day, once the LP and concert film were released. But while the stars of Woodstock were as much the sea of bodies caked in mud, the rolling farmland, and the peace-love ethic as they were the performers on a distant stage, the champion of the Garden that afternoon was indisputably Harrison—for his stardom, and for his sheer charisma, artistic and political, as a pop culture figure. He sustained the tone of the show—solemnly purposeful but engagingly loose—with a master stroke of audience control: he knew enough to acknowledge his Beatle past for the fans who came to celebrate it with him in person, but he resisted any temptation to exploit it for any private star-tripping needs. Unlike Woodstock, there was no mellower-than-thou self-congratulation, and if Woodstock's ultimate aims were collectively narcissistic, the concerts for Bangla Desh were strenuously humanitarian and, where money was concerned, all but "egoless," many performers cancelling paying dates on two continents to fly in for the benefit shows.

That afternoon stands as the high point of Harrison's career, and in a sense it symbolizes its complex nature. Here was Harrison, a master in the material world of superstars, managers, money, and music, acting like an aural prism onstage, collecting some pure light of inspiration and scattering it across the stage into virtually every coloration of popular music from the preceding decade: English blues-rock; American folk; American rock; gospel-rooted R & B; Indian ragas; rockabilly. Included as well was the crisp efficiency of L.A. sessions men who were faceless superstars on dozens of hit records forming the new L.A. rock industry; and of course, the two most dynamic forces in music during the 60s, the

Beatles and Dylan. But if the concerts defined Harrison's pre-eminence among the mighty—and mortal—in rock, they also linked him, through Shankar, his sitar, and his people, to the roots of his own immersion in Hindu philosophy and religion, and his own "God-realization" through Krishna consciousness.

The concerts presented us with the odd, deep symmetry in his career, the simultaneous presence of the material and spiritual. Few figures in popular music could generate so prodigious a sum of money by assembling such a show, and Harrison's weeks of work paid off in millions of dollars to save lives and relieve the suffering of a people who were indirectly tied to his own spiritual rebirth and subsequent strenuous de-mythification as a Beatle. Here was George Harrison singing "Beware of maya," all illusion, "as each unconscious sufferer wanders aimlessly," warning his fans about material attachments, urging them to look beyond appearance to find the one divine consciousness in all of us—but he was speaking to people who had helped make him one of the most celebrated and wealthy folk heroes of his time. After a five-year absence from the concert stage, it was clear that, as far as the material world was concerned, George Harrison was thriving within it and without it.

Joseph Sia.
Madison Square
Garden, 1974

Previous page:
Ken Regan/Camera 5.
The end of the
Bangladesh event,
Madison Square
Garden

FROM LIVERPOOL
TO 'LET IT BE'

2 More than any other Beatle, George Harrison was emotionally cushioned through childhood and adolescence by a large and close-knit family. As a boy, John Lennon hardly knew his father, Fred; saw his mother, Julia, only occasionally, and was raised by his Aunt Mimi; then in his teens, when for the first time in his life he was becoming attached to his mother, who had been living nearby in Liverpool, she was killed by a car while crossing a street—a brutally scarring trauma. Paul McCartney enjoyed the intimacy and security of a happy family life until his mother died barely a month after a diagnosis of cancer. He was 14 at the time and the shock of her death, his brother Mike recalled in Hunter Davies' intimate account, *The Beatles, The Authorized Biography,* propelled Paul into a melancholic escape through guitar playing. And Ringo, an only child, like John, was raised by his struggling mother after she was divorced from his father, whom he hardly knew. Ringo grew up, by his own description, a lonely and often sickly child.

George's home, though, was a swirl of good-natured family fun. He was the third son and fourth child of Harold and Louise Harrison, born in February 1943. The Harrisons lived in Liverpool's Wavertree section, near John's and Paul's homes. Harold Harrison had been a merchant marine for ten years before he quit in the mid-30s to come home to be with his family more. He worked on cruise ships, he told Davies, and often tried to boost his 25-shilling-a-week pay with big tips from the "good bloods" on board, and with part-time haircutting jobs. He provided the family with a modest terrace house, but once back on land he found the going rough—spending more than a year on dole and eventually driving a city bus. As a young child, Mrs. Harrison told Davies, George was independent from the start, and could run errands for her without a shopping list. When it came time to enroll at primary school, George, unlike most other kids, never bawled at the school gates, never even wanted to come home for lunch. When he was six, the family moved up socially into government-subsidized housing, and George recalled to Davies the thrill of a more spacious home. "It seemed fantastic. You could go from that hall to the sitting room, then into the kitchen, then into hall again, and back into the sitting room. I just ran around and around it all the first day."

Soon, though, the novelty wore off; things looked tougher. Neighborhood kids picked fights, destroyed his mom's plants and flowers, and were indifferent or distracting at school. By the age of nine, enrolled at Liverpool Institute, the city's top grammar school, George was ducking homework as cagily as he ducked fights. He grew to resist—and resent—authority figures at school, who he said to Davies "were just trying to turn everybody into little rows of toffees."

McCartney, meanwhile, was a year ahead of George at the Institute, and Lennon was well on to Quarry Bank High School. George gradually found flashy clothes a suitable way of expressing hostility toward teachers—outrageously tight pants, wildly flamboyant shirts—but reached a sort of detente with them: "I had this mutual thing with a few masters," Davies was told. "They'd let me sleep at the back of the class and I wouldn't cause any trouble. If it was nice and sunny, it was hard to keep awake anyway, with some old fellow chundering away on. I often used to wake up at quarter to five and find they'd all gone home long ago."

At 14, George found an even better way to deal with anger: playing the guitar. His first one, a 3 gift from his mother, came from a school friend after he asked his mom for it. And his parents were always supportive in his growing interest in music, which then was focused squarely on skiffle music. This was a folk-derived music played with acoustic guitars, string basses, and washboards. John, Paul, and George were all fans of one skiffle star in particular, Lonnie Donegan, who had a U.S. hit in the 50s titled "Does Your Chewing Gum Lose Its Flavor on the Bedpost Overnight?" Jaunty, chordally simple, skiffle intrigued George because he could graft the chord formations from records or manuals onto his own primitive guitar, and work on new chords well into the night, often with his mom by his side to lend encouragement.

George played one concert with a band named (for one night only) the

Opposite:
The Quarrymen in Liverpool, 1958

Rebels, but more importantly, was deepening a friendship with a sweet-faced lad from the Institute who often rode the school bus with him, Paul McCartney. When their shared affection for skiffle died down with the genre itself, they both were drawn instinctively to the American rock and roll music they heard on records by Elvis Presley, Chuck Berry, Jerry Lee Lewis, Carl Perkins, and Little Richard. Paul was asked to join a local band that included John Lennon on guitar about a year after Paul and George became friends. The band was called the Quarrymen, and George, though considerably younger than John, was invited in about one year later, in 1958. Despite George's insecure feelings about John's wit and intellectualism and his savvy Art Institute companions, George quickly proved to be a more dexterous and curious guitarist. He would develop new chord patterns and show them to Lennon and McCartney, who would then try to construct a melody around the chords. Those three, plus a turnover of extra guitarists, drummers, and bassists, played local parties, but rarely got paid except in sodas and plates of beans. But to George it must have looked promising—at age 16, in 1959, he formally quit Liverpool Institute.

To earn money he found himself a day job as an electrician's apprentice, but soon quit as he "Kept blowin' things up." The Quarrymen were thickening their rock and roll beat, improving on their amplification equipment, and slowly filling in nights with gigs at Liverpool civic halls, social clubs, and bus depots, according to Davies. Later in 1959 they added Stu Sutcliffe, John's Art Institute friend, on bass, and toured Scotland for two weeks as the Silver Beatles. Except for their first autograph signings and the first taste of road life, it was an uneventful trip, and it lead to an anticlimactic return home to low-life strip joints, "Teddy boys," workers, and general bar-band misery. The following year, though, they signed Pete Best on drums, whose mother owned the Cavern club in Liverpool. The five musicians then signed for a booking in Hamburg, their first outside the U.K. The Indra club was oppressive, dismal, a wretched place for young, wide-eyed teenagers. Hamburg, a

At the Cavern Club, 1961

16

tough, rainy, cold port city with crime, whores, drunken sailors, and hoodlums in the streets, was much like Liverpool, but worse in every way. They were camped out in the unheated Bambi Cinema, which was so awful they played as long as possible at the club just to avoid coming home to the movie house. They were expanding their repertoire too, but the club was folding, and they moved on to the Kaiserkeller. There, they developed their reputation for providing high-energy rock for 12 hours on end, and soon they became the rage of Hamburg's seedy Reeperbahn, its 42nd Street. This five-month engagement signalled their first experiences with pep pills and other stimulants, but *nothing* could keep them going when, suddenly, George was deported for being underage at drinking spots, and then Paul and Pete were shipped home for inadvertently starting a fire in the Bambi as they were moving their belongings to a new and classier club, the Top Ten, where they had just agreed to play.

Back in Liverpool again, they returned to the steamy clubs frequented by leather-jacketed Teds and their tough-talking birds. But the Beatles were delivering something new on the British music front, which until then had been made up largely of soporific pop, even at its best. They played a music, as their American heroes did, that incited the youth, whipped them into a manic excitement, made them shake and unified them. They were becoming known, and in early 1961 they became the headlining, or resident, group at Liverpool's showcase club, the Cavern. It was a glorious time of intimate identification with their audiences: ''We were playing to our own fans,'' George told Davies. ''They were like us. They would come in at lunchtime to hear us and bring their sandwiches to eat instead of having lunch. We would do the same, eating our lunch while we played. It was just spontaneous.''

By the end of 1961 the Beatles were shuttling between two home bases, the Top Ten and the Cavern. During one booking at the Top Ten, Sutcliffe decided to leave the band to pursue his art studies. It was then that Paul assumed the chores on bass, and George, though more serious and less animated than the others, became the

The Beatles, 1962, and Brian Epstein (inset)

fulltime lead guitarist. (Sutcliffe died a year later of a brain hemorrhage.)

The cult of the Mersey beat was beginning to open up back in Liverpool, and gossip columns began charting the Beatles' every move. Their first fan club was formed in late 1961. When a Liverpool Beatle fan requested their German-made single record, ''My Bonnie,'' in a classy Liverpool record shop at the end of the year, the Beatles were unaware that they were getting their biggest break. The store manager was 27-year-old Brian Epstein, and he was determined, out of sound business practices, rather than love of the music, to track it down for his customer. He found it, ordered 200 copies for his store, and when he sold all of them in a very short time, he knew something special was going on. After several meetings with them, he decided to sign them up to a management contract that guaranteed him 25 percent of their earnings off the top. In return, he assured them his close contacts in the record industry would lead to a recording contract. But that end of the deal seemed to sag right off.

They failed a dismal audition at Decca Records, as well as numerous others through the spring of 1962. Then Epstein got them a hearing with George Martin, the producer at Parlophone, whose parent company, E.M.I., had already passed on a chance to sign with the Beatles. Martin, a dapper, patrician man, was sufficiently intrigued by Paul's warbling and George's clear lead-guitar lines to ask them to record, still as an audition, one song: they cut ''Love Me Do'' in June 1962. A month later, in the midst of a heavy performing schedule which earned them a top figure of £85 a week they learned that Martin would sign them to Parlophone.

Just as they were about to get off the ground, drummer Pete Best, either at Martin's suggestion or Epstein's urging, was asked to leave the group. It caused a bitter controversy within the group, but there was the first recording to look to, and they quickly replaced Best with a solemn-faced drummer for the local group Rory Storm and the Hurricanes: Ringo Starr. Starr had actually sat in with the Beatles during their gigs in Hamburg, when his band was in town, and he got on particularly well with George. Everyone agreed he was the top drum-

Ringo was hired as drummer at the end of 1964

mer around and a natural choice for the band.

The Fab Four—the configuration that would soon erupt on the world of music—was formed and ready to make their music for the record. Still moving back and forth between live shows in Hamburg and Liverpool, they re-cut ''Love Me Do'' toward the end of 1962, and then their follow-up, ''Please Please Me.'' ''Love Me Do'' did well, not extraordinarily well, on the pop charts, but in February 1963 ''Please Please Me'' shot to number one on English charts, and they were off and sprinting to glory. They did their first national tour that spring, with pop singer Helen Shapiro as headliner, and cut their first LP, *Please Please Me;* in April, their second big hit, ''From Me to You,'' from the LP, reached number one. The commercial explosion that would accompany Beatlemania had begun—the start of a long string of number-one single records and more than a *dozen* topselling LPs between mid-1963 and November 1967.

The Beatles toured as co-headliner with American rock star Roy Orbison in mid-1963, and by then, almost any utterance by a Beatle was assured of being magnified and distorted in headlines across England. After six tireless years of obscurity they were suddenly being sucked into a violent whirlpool of notoriety, crazy public scrutiny, hysteria, wealth, and, ultimately, exhaustion. They were being ripped from their moorings in Liverpool and

*Opposite:
Rex Features.
In the Cavern,
early 1963*

would soon be tossed into the deep, treacherous international waters of mass merchandising, worldwide touring, and unprecedented planetary adulation. There was a television show viewed by 15 million in England; their first airport riot in October 1963; their legendary appearance at the Royal Variety Performance, at which John instructed the stuffy blue-bloods to rattle their jewelry in time to the pounding rhythms. These were all the early seismic tremors that signalled the cultural earthquake of Beatlemania.

By the end of 1963 their single "I Want to Hold Your Hand" had incredible advance orders of one million

copies, four times Elvis Presley's largest advance order for a single. Journalists were crawling for access with the Beatles, the group's offices had been shifted to London, and England's prestigious New Musical Express voted them the world's top group.

Then, the American invasion: Murray the K's manic radio interviews from their hotel rooms, which brought their individual and distinct characters into shape. John, the sarcastic, intellectual one; Paul, the sweetly earnest and cutest one; Ringo, the monotoned, cranky, deadpan funnyman; and George, the Quiet One, the inscrutable one who seemed in pictures to squint through his teeth when he managed a smile. They were charmingly aloof, daringly irreverent;

and if they seemed to own the world, they did. The Beatles made history at Carnegie Hall—as much for the mass hysteria as for the brevity of their show, about 37 minutes long—and their "Ed Sullivan Show" appearance captivated some 73 million Americans. In March 1964, advance orders for their single "Can't Buy Me Love" soared to an unimaginable three million copies.

They paused from this promotional grind just long enough to shoot *A Hard Day's Night* in the spring of 1964. George met a London model named Patti Boyd on the set of the film. She was in it because its director, Richard Lester, had shot her in a TV ad he had produced in London. She was beautiful, blonde, from a middle-class family in southern England. From that point on, George and Patti dated constantly and she moved in to share his sprawling white bungalow in Esher, England, in late 1964. But before they could hold a home life together—as was the case throughout much of the next three years—the Beatles hit the road again, this time for their first major worldwide tour on the Continent, across the United States, and through other countries. For three years, until late summer of 1966, the Beatles spent a tremendous amount of time on the road—three major tours each year, playing record crowds in huge American baseball stadiums, generating record ticket grosses, ($304,000 for one show), and receiving record guarantees for large outdoor shows ($150,000 from a baseball owner in Kansas City named Charles Finley).

But by the summer of 1966, having cranked out, incredibly, dozens of singles and a dozen LPs, shot two Beatle films, and toured the world at least three times, they all began to sense something had to give. The strain and depression, the disorientation of air travel over weeks at a time, the endless string of hotels and room service meals—it all began to turn their lives from a dizzying fantasy to a nightmare of hollow fame. Instead of reaching their fans through live shows, the Beatles felt they were growing more insulated from them. They lived under perpetual house arrest at hotels, and their sense of time and space eroded as tours wore on. With no monitoring equipment onstage— or at least inadequate equipment—their

21

playing was deteriorating. Maybe not. They couldn't tell, and their fans couldn't care. They had too little time to explore their musical directions in the studio, and worse, they realized the quality of their work made absolutely no difference to their fans, who, it seemed, would buy anything from the Beatles. To salvage their musical integrity, in a sense, to allow John and Paul to develop more as writers than as rock stars, they withdrew from live performing at the conclusion of their summer 1966 tour. The last U.S. date they played was at San Francisco's Candlestick Park in August of that year.

The Beatles needed six years to ignite as a touring group, three years for the fuse to burn, and, once the explosion was over, two years to burn out. Their private lives were scattered, and unlike most of their fans, they were no longer teenagers. George, the youngest, was 23 when they retired from live touring. All but Paul were married, and two had children. ''We got in a rut,'' said a world-weary Harrison. ''It was like the end of a cycle. It was a different audience every night but we did the same songs

every night. Nobody could hear. There was no satisfaction in it at all. It was just a bloody big row. We got worse as musicians, playing the same old junk every day.''

More than the others, Harrison had a personal and passionate non-Beatle pursuit in mind when he quit the road. While on the set for *Help,* in 1965, he idly picked up a peculiar-looking stringed instrument left there to lend

Previous page:
Jim Marshall.

an exotic appearance. The sound of this instrument, the sitar, suggested the snow-capped peaks of the Himalayas, the endless rolling plains of India; it suggested a serene and mystical allure far beyond the fainting, foaming crowds, the moneymen, the road crews, the limos, the hotel rooms. Harrison must have first picked up the sitar, strummed it a few times, and, one can imagine, think he had just played the lead guitar of Paradise. This was sometime between February and May of 1965. Five months later, he would add a buzzing brush-stroke to the song "Norwegian Wood," a haunting sitar-effect that helped spur him on to study the extremely complex and hypnotizing instrument.

The communality of Beatle life had in a way stunted Harrison's growth—emotional, musical—as it had for the others. But George was only 15 when he joined, hardly a seasoned young man, and the end of touring was the first real opportunity to catch up on lost time and to get into something for himself, to go back to where his life had left off, in a sense, and start over as George Harrison.

"After 'Norwegian Wood,' " he has said, "I met Ravi Shankar at a friend's house in London, for dinner. He offered to give me instructions in the basics of the sitar, like how to sit, how to hold it, and the basic exercises. It was the first time I had ever really learned music with a bit of discipline. Then I started to listen to Indian music for the next two years, and hardly touched the guitar, except for recordings. Having all these material things, I wanted something more. And it happened that at just the time I wanted it, it came to me in the form of Ravi Shankar, Indian

Camera 5.
George meets
Ravi Shankar,
1966

music, and the whole Indian philosophy.'' Harrison and his wife Patti were determined to track it all down, and after the 1966 summer tour ended, they left for a two-month trip through India. George placed himself at the feet of the master for intensive sitar instruction, and was thoroughly absorbed in the entire experience. ''I went partly to learn music and partly to see and learn as much as I could about India as possible. I'd always heard stories about men in caves in the Himalayas, hundreds of years old, and people who can levitate and people who get buried under the ground for six weeks and lots of what the West would call mysticism. But when you get there you find that this is happening all over the place, with people materializing left, right and center. I know everybody has a different interpretation of God, but whatever identity—in cosmic terms. ''Here everybody is vibrating on a material level which is nowhere. Over there, they have this great feeling of something else that's just spiritual going on. Once you get to the point where you really believe that you're trying to do things for the truth, then nobody can touch you because you're harmonizing with a great power. The more into this spiritual thing I go, the more I realize that we're not doing it—the Beatles—but that something else is doing it.''

Harrison's trip included long discussions with some 200 of Shankar's students, many of whom study years before giving up their formal training, and an eye-opening trip to a religious festival along the bank of the Ganges River. More than anything else, he learned a new time-phase, a new rhythm to life on earth and beyond, and a profound sense of humility from

God is, by becoming one with that you naturally discover every sort of law that governs. That's why people like Jesus can make these sort of miracles.''

Looking back a year later Harrison saw that this trip to India led to his first profound reassessment of his Beatle

Shankar himself: ''He sat down, this great master giant of a man on the sitar, and showed me scales the first lesson.''

The summer of 1966 was also the approximate date of George's first experiences with LSD, which he first took unknowingly at the home of a

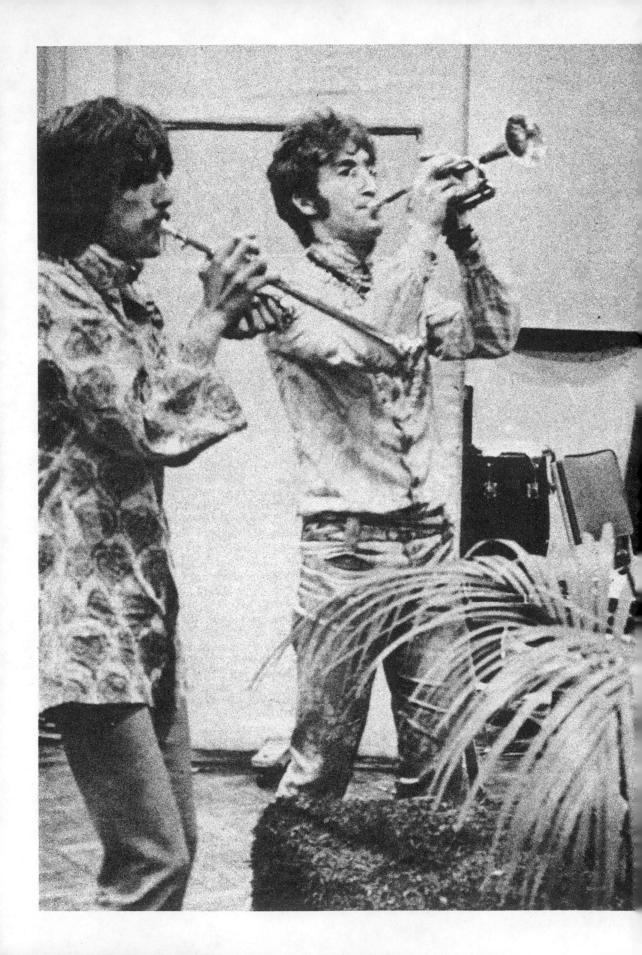

*Sergeant Pepper's
Lonely Hearts
Club Band*

dentist friend of John Lennon's. There were at least several more acid trips by the early months of 1967, around the time the Beatles were recording *Sgt. Pepper's Lonely Hearts Club Band*. Drugs, like the sitar, could become a tool in the spiritual explorations he was undertaking, but never an end in themselves.

"It was like I had never tasted, smelled, heard anything before," he said of his first LSD trips. "For me it was like a flash. It just opened something inside of me and I realized a lot of things," he told editor Mitchell Glazer of *Crawdaddy*. "I didn't learn them, because I already knew them, but that happened to be the key that opened the door to reveal them. From the moment I had that I wanted to have it all the time—these thoughts about the yogis, and the Himalayas, and Ravi's music." Once he got into meditation and Krishna chanting, he would later say, it helped him handle the pressures of his musical career much more easily: "You either go crackers and commit suicide, or you try and use every incident in order to realize something and attach yourself more strongly to an inner strength." It helps me rise above the heaviness we've all gone through and are still

going through. It's all part of maya."

Harrison's most powerful musical and philosophical account of his then young search for God and enlightenment was his "Within You Without You," on *Sgt. Pepper*. The whole album was momentously catalytic in the context of cultural upheaval of the mid-60s, amidst the holocaust of Vietnam and the coming drug culture. The LP's effect swept through virtually all aspects of the American culture at that time, and seemed to usher in new styles of slang, dress, music of course, and social behavior. There was a summing up of the sense of futility and outrage over the world's events ("I read the news today, oh boy"); the sadness and insincerity of parent-child relations in conditions of material well-being ("Sacrificed most of our lives . . .we gave her everything money could buy"); and it provided an informal license to use drugs as a means fo fully savor the imagaic hedonism of psychedelic vision: ("tangerine trees and marmalade skies"). But beyond it all lay Harrison's mind-blower, his immortally droned chant, with sitar and tabla accompaniment: "We were talking, about the space between us all, and the people who hide behind a

34

wall of illusion never glimpse the truth.'' Then he asks abruptly, ''Are you one of them?'' Now, this was not only a soundtrack for the counterculture ethos—which divided people by age (the breaking point was 30), dress, values, and other abstract factors of hipness and political thought and action—but for something more profound. For Harrison went beyond, and extended his vision all the way through the galaxies, dividing the spiritually graceful and spiritually lame. Granola may have become the breakfast of America's new anti-champions and anti-capitalists, but Harrison was saying that style itself, whatever form it takes, is but illusion, not an attachment that matters.

The LP was massively unifying for the youth, and was, in the words of Langdon Winner, ''the closest thing Western civilization has come to unity since the Congress of Vienna . . . . For a brief while, the irreparably fragmented consciousness of the West was unified, at least in the minds of the young.''

But not necessarily in the minds of the Beatles. Even as the hippies of Haight-Ashbury were developing a hard-core acid culture around *Sgt. Pepper* and other San Francisco groups like the Jefferson Airplane and Grateful Dead, the Beatles' drug days were ending. In fact, the album marks the end of Beatlemania, and the beginning of the deep centrifugal forces that would tear the Fab Four apart. ''Still, if *Sgt. Pepper* was an ending,'' Greil Marcus wrote in the *Rolling Stone Illustrated History of Rock & Roll,* ''it was an ending that has never been matched.''

Significantly, at the height of the *Sgt. Pepper* explosion Harrison and his wife visited the Haight-Ashbury section of San Francisco. Harrison, in heart-shaped sunglasses, flowered trowsers, and a denim jacket with a button reading ''I'm HEAD of my household,'' asked to borrow a guitar from some youth, and strummed the chords and sang to ''How Does It Feel to Be One of the Beautiful People?'' Asked later how he found the hippies, Harrison disapprovingly likened them to another social force he had helped set in motion, and disliked—Beatlemania: ''It's a great idea and there are lots of great people but there are always the bad that accompanies the good. I got the impression it's a craze,

a little like Beatlemania. For some it's as if they've got their hippie rule book which they abide by, but don't really feel it. I realized that non-conforming is actually conforming to a new form.''

The Harrisons' trip to Hippieland did fuel their interest in the exoticism of the East, however, and in the late summer of 1967, through Patti, who had read about him, George and the other Beatles decided to meet Maharishi Mahesh Yogi at a conference in Wales. They were joined by Mick Jagger, Marianne Faithful, and Jennie Boyd, Patti's sister, also a London model. Brian Epstein had planned to come for the weekend, but stayed at his home in Sussex with two friends. On the second day of the retreat, they received word that Epstein had died from a drug overdose, presumably by accident. The Beatles recoiled immediately, and left the retreat. With their manager's death, it was as if the ma-

Ethan Russell. The beginning of the deep forces that would tear the fab four apart

terial, corporate side of them was gone, the single strongest unifying influence of the group for many years.

To Harrison it must have confirmed on some deep level what he had begun to feel potently in himself, that the world of material well-being is transitory, illusory, mortal. The Beatles held on, barely, to put together their chaotic and critically savaged *Magical Mystery Tour,* and then in early 1968, did make a pilgrimage to the Maharishi's ashram in Rishikesh. But their cynicism and disillusionment soon embraced the giddy guru himself, when it was widely believed that he and actress Mia Farrow, another disciple, were communing on a patently secular basis. Lennon informed the Maharishi that the Beatles' interest in him was terminated, and according to the authors of *Apple to the Core,* Peter McCabe and Robert Shonfeld, ''the Beatles had learned nothing from the experience with the Maharishi. They felt they had been made to look fools.''

Harrison retreated into the sitar more deeply than ever, until the sessions for *The Beatles* (or the White Album) in 1968. It was the first time during recording sessions that at least two beatles, Harrison and Ringo, actually left the sessions to think things over. There was also, no co-written material. Harrison had all but lost interest in his instrument, but as he was developing a close friendship with Cream's super-fluid blues interpreter, Eric Clapton, he slowly came back to the guitar—encouraged by a gift Clapton made of a Les Paul guitar, a favorite among many rock stars.

Harrison was suddenly curious on the instrument again: ''I was a bit rusty, since we gave up live playing. I always wanted to catch up on my playing. And there were all these eight-year-old kids comin' up with the best licks you ever heard. I started at that time too to play the slide guitar.'' This was a technique of gently gliding a glass or metal cylinder encasing the pinky or ring finger along the steel strings of an electric guitar, to create a flowing, ethereal string of notes, or a rich, gliding chord sequence. (Clapton, Duane Allman of the Allman Brothers Band, Keith Richard of the Rolling Stones, and Harrison became the leading stylists in this technique by 1970, each with a distinct and identifiable sound.)

After the White Album, Harrison's frustrations as a songwriter and confinement as a guitarist grew more severe, amidst the complicated lawsuits to gain control over the Beatles' publishing and corporate empire. The struggle was waged eventually between McCartney, who favored his in-laws, the Eastman family, to run the Beatles' money show, and the other three, who favored rock industry wheeler-dealer Allen Klein. Harrison, meanwhile, was moonlighting frequently on projects for other artists, playing or producing.

Though the Beatles came together to record *Abbey Road, Let It Be,* and the material for *Hey Jude* and *Yellow Submarine,* effectively, they had all but ceased to function as a working group. In April 1970, a month before their final group release, *Let It Be,* McCartney announced he was leaving the group, angered over the appointment of Klein as manager of Apple Ltd., the omnibus corporation for their business and record label (Apple). It hardly mattered at that point. The split-up was a formality. Harrison had been pursuing adulterous artistic relationships with numerous American musicians in L.A., had spent a Thanksgiving in Woodstock, jammed with Bob Dylan, and above all, was lifting off the years of restless limitation by Lennon and McCartney and sensing out his own musical directions. He had been busy and free, but when he returned to the studio for the taping of *Let It Be* (not their last session, which were the *Abbey Road* sessions), he hit a brick wall. ''I was in a very happy frame of mind, but I quickly

discovered I was up against the same old Paul,'' he told McCabe and Shonfeld. "In front of the cameras as we were actually being filmed, Paul started to get at me about the way I was playing. I was starting to enjoy being a musician again, but the moment I got back with the Beatles it was too difficult. Everyone was sort of pigeon-holed.''

"They automatically thought their tunes should get the priority, so for me I'd always have to wait for ten songs of theirs before they'd even listen to one of mine,'' he told Mitchell Glazer. "It was like I'd been constipated. I had a little encouragement from time to time, but it was like they were doing me a favor. I didn't have much confidence in writing songs because of that.''

The Beatles dream was ending, but their final releases reflected none of the dissension or dwindling velocity as a group and social force. At least not on record charts. *Sgt. Pepper* ran an incredible 15 weeks as number one, according to *Billboard* listings, in the summer of 1967, and remained in the top ten for 33 weeks. *Magical Mystery Tour,* conceded to be a fiasco on film and record (there are virtually no guitar solos or standout riffs), shot from number 157 to number 4 its second week on the charts, and stuck at number one for 8 weeks and top ten for 14. *The Beatles* hit number one for 10 weeks and top ten for 15; *Abbey Road* shot from 178 to 4 its second charted week, stuck at number one for 11 weeks, and lingered in the top ten an incredible 27 weeks. *Hey Jude,* a collection of unreleased material and some singles, never hit number one but was top ten for 11 weeks—though the single, "Hey Jude," their stunning seven-minute classic, towered at number one on singles charts for an amazing run of two months. *Yellow Submarine,* six Beatle cuts and a side of George Martin orchestrations for the animated film was top ten for 6 weeks. *Let It Be* reached number one for 4 weeks, and top ten for 10. In fact, according to the thoroughly detailed account of the Beatles' entire recording career, *All Together Now,* compiled by Harry Castleman and

Alan Howard. George gravitates toward Ravi and the sitar

Walter J. Podrazik, five Beatle LPs were all on pop charts simultaneously in July 1970. And while it is common for a new release to spur interest in an artist's ''catalogue,'' those Beatle LPs were all released within a three-year period and *still* selling briskly. Even as the sun was setting on the Beatle empire, in the final week of 1970, three of their LPs were on the charts—as were solo albums by each of the Beatles, including George's commercial triumph *All Things Must Pass*. That same week it entered the *Billboard* listings as number two, an extremely rare feat in itself, to begin a run of 9 weeks in the top five. Ironically, it seemed that in their death as a group the Beatles had birthed a new and all but unknown artist. 🍎

Bottom:
UPI Photo.
Pete Bennet of
Apple Corps and
Phil Spector
(producer) listen
to the final mix
of "All Things
Must Pass", New
York, 1961

COMMUTING TO THE MATERIAL WORLD

3 By the end of 1970 when McCartney sued the Beatles to dissolve their partnership, only George among them was a non-parent. This could have been due either to the stability of his early home life, which may have diminished any need for a nuclear family security, or simply because of his desire to flourish as an artist and spiritualist without complex domestic obligations. Harrison had indeed pursued his musical and spiritual interests with gusto between 1968 and 1970, despite the traumatic dissolving of the greatest single group in pop music history.

After their ill-fated trip to the Maharishi's ashram in early 1968, Harrison and Patti retreated to their white, psychedelically painted bungalow in Esher, one place they felt sure to be able to live private lives, pursue meditation and chanting, and for George, still be close to the London music scene. The home was painted in dayglo, a popular effect of the late 60s hippie culture—swirls of abstract designs, cartoons and flowers, all done by George (who also put the brush to his Mini automobile). But the flamboyance of the outside of the home was balanced by the comparatively subdued atmosphere of the living room. There were low benches and leather cushions on the floor, in North African or Middle Eastern style—no chairs, just the leather cushions. The home was nestled in a wooded garden, secluded and invisible from the road. As was customary for years, there would usually be incense burning somewhere within the house, helping to create a soft, contemplatively serene mood. Harrison was approaching at this time new depths of negativism toward his Beatle karma: "I don't really enjoy being a Beatle anymore," he confided to Davies. "It's trivial, it's unimportant. I'm fed up with all this me, us, I stuff and all the meaningless things we do. I'm trying to work out solutions to the more important things in life. Thinking about being a Beatle is going backwards. I'm concerned more with the future. It would take me six months to explain all the things I believe in—all the Hindu theories, the Eastern philosophies, reincarnation, transcendental meditation. It's when you begin to understand those things that you realize how pointless the other stuff is."

Despite his warnings, Harrison essayed an explanation of some of his beliefs: "It's basically a cosmic vision in which life on earth is but a fleeting illusion edged between lives past and future beyond physical mortal reality. We've all been here before. I don't know what as. You go on being reincarnated until you reach the actual Truth. Heaven and Hell are just a state of mind. We are all here to become Christ-like. The actual world is an illusion. I'm beginning to know that all I know is that I know nothing."

Long before the breakup of the Beatles, Harrison involved himself in solo projects as writer, player, and producer, and was the most active Beatle moonlighter. In early 1968, before the trip to India, he wrote a little-known Beatle single called "The Inner Light," using Indian musicians. The song reflected his philosophical bent at the time. The instrumental tracks were recorded in a Bombay studio, and while he was there Harrison also cut the Indian instrumentals for his haunting and ambitious LP, *Wonderwall Music,* also a soundtrack for a film. He wrote all the musical parts for Indian and Western musicians and produced the LP, a non-commercial avant-garde venture that whetted his taste for fusing Indian music and religion with his own Western tastes. He also learned to rough it a bit while at the Bombay sessions: "It was fantastic, really. The studio's on top of the offices but there's no sound proofing. So if you listen closely to some of the Indian tracks on the LP you can hear taxis going by. Every time the offices knocked off at 5:30 we had to stop recording because you could just hear everybody stomping down the steps. They only had a big old E.M.I. mono machine. It was too incredible. I mixed everything as we did it. It was nice enough because you get spoiled working on eight and sixteen tracks."

And while he was recording the White Album, from May through October, 1968, according to the *All Together Now* compendium, Harrison took time out to record one of his own compositions, "Sour Milk Sea," for a Jackie Lomax Apple LP, and joined Clapton in the studio to play guitar on a tune he co-wrote with him, "Badge," which was included on the *Goodbye*

Opposite:
Jeffrey Mayer/
Rainbow.
Isle of Wight,
1969

Previous page:
Ken Regan/Camera 5.

Cream LP. Then from October 1968 through early weeks of 1969, he sat in the control booth and produced the rest of Lomax's album, *Is This What You Want?* In November 1968 he wrote and produced half of another bizarre and noncommercial LP called *Electronic Sound*, and completed it in early 1969.

The spring of 1969 was a busy one, not only in the studios, but in court-rooms. Harrison was fined $200 for assaulting a photographer at the Cannes Film Festival, and in March, his home was raided by a group of policemen whose dope-sniffing was the biggest stick of hash I have ever seen and obviously I'd have known about it if I'd seen it before. Those who think this is a low down dirty thing to smoke pot will be further convinced they're right and we're wrong. But it will strengthen the others who follow us. We were once every-body's darlings. But it isn't like that anymore. They hate us.'' (Harrison, like Lennon after his drug possession conviction, could never get a visa to come and stay in the U.S. to work, until his major concert tour in 1974.)

More somber, feeling harassed and vulnerable in their bungalow, the

Apis/Camera 5.

police dogs allegedly dug up some 570 grains of marijuana—enough, the police charged, for at least 120 joints. The same week that John and Yoko Lennon spent in bed for world peace in Amsterdam, George and Patti Harrison were walking out of a magistrate's court in London, slapped with a £ 600 fine. Harrison pleaded to reporters: ''We hope the police will now leave the Beatles alone. I just want to be left alone to be a free individual to pursue my own work.'' And he added, ''Why did they have to arrest me on Paul McCartney's wed-ding day?'' Harrison protested the drugs had been planted: ''I'm a tidy sort of bloke. I don't like chaos. I kept records in the records rack, tea on the tea caddy, and pot in the pot box. This Harrisons decided to move, commen-cing a year-long search for the dream house. What they found in March 1970 was Friar Park, 35 acres in Henley-on-Thames, a massive 30-room Gothic mansion with gargoyles, gnome sta-tues, stained glass windows, and three interconnected underground lakes. The gorgeous setting cost $336,000, but it offered seclusion and peacefulness, the most important fac-tors in trying to set up a normal life-style. Patti and her sister were able to further involve themselves in Hindu literature, to take dancing lessons, and study, in Patti's case, an Indian instrument for a while. Meanwhile, George—before, during, and after the *Abbey Road* sessions, from early June to August 1969—was putting his

Opposite:
With Ravi Shankar
in India

emancipation drive in full gear. He produced several chants with devotees from the Radha Krishna Temple of London in the summer of 1969; played guitar (as L'Angelo Mysterioso) on a Jack Bruce single; and produced Billy Preston's LP, *That's the Way God Planned It.* Toward the end of the year he produced another Preston cut, a Lomax cut, and a song for singer Doris Troy, and in January 1970 produced several more chants with Krishna devotees from the London temple. In the spring of the same year he produced yet another Preston LP, *Encouraging Words.* In June, he recorded a guitar track on "Tell the Truth" for Clapton's landmark LP, *Layla* (as Derek and the Dominoes), which

brought together such session all-stars as Bobby Whitlock (keyboard), Jim Gordon (drums), Carl Radle (bass), and on other cuts, the slide guitar genius of Duane Allman. Harrison was surrounding himself in these studio sessions with top players of all kinds of music—funk-rock, slick L.A. rock, English blues, Southern rock, and even Indian chanting—and his interests were widening rapidly.

Widening too was his involvement with the London Krishna temple during the period of relative calm and domestic tranquility in the new home. In late 1969 and early 1970 Harrison would phone up the temple in London and invite several young devotees out to his manor for chanting and discus-

sions of Krishna consciousness. This was the path Harrison had chosen as a means of God-realization, a simple practice of chanting Hare Krishna regularly with prayer beads. He had met and now could converse freely with His Divine Grace A.C. Bhaktivedanta Prabhupada, the founder of the International Society for Krishna Consciousness, a man Harrison has said was enormously influential in his development. Or on other occasions Harrison would drop by the temple, in jeans and a shirt, and discuss Krishna and Hindu philosophy with the devotees. There was never a "cult of personality" around him in these informal gatherings, and that facilitated Harrison's relations with them. For several months a small group of devotees actually lived with the Harrisons at Friar Park, waking up early to begin the day-long chanting. Sometimes George would play the harmonium, a small droning keyboard instrument that can maintain a major chord while chanters sing along in harmonic accompaniment. The chants consisted of short, repetitive phrases like *Hare Krishna, Hare Rama Rama Rama,* or *Jai Jai Govinda.* Some would close their eyes slightly, finger their prayer beads and experience a deeply relaxing physical and spiritual high. Despite the pressures to record with the Beatles or any other artists, Harrison not only found time for but seemed to actually relish these intimate and private meetings with his spiritual brothers and sisters. To open himself up to others in so revealing and unifying a way was clearly a profound pleasure for the superstar, whose privacy had for so long been invaded—or at least limited—by the press, fans, and in a different way, the other Beatles. George was finding a way to cut through all the elitism, suspiciousness, and aloofness that so many of his professional colleagues foster at the top of their careers. Best of all, he found beyond it, a sense of divine indivisible Oneness with all being.

"The phone rang one afternoon at the temple," one devotee recalled of that period. "The president of the temple answered the phone. He stood there and just smiled. He didn't say anything at all. Then he hung up and smiled broadly. I asked him what had happened. 'That was George,' he told me. 'He called from Henley. He is in bliss. He has been chanting for the last 14 hours.''

Harrison expressed some of his growing love for the Krishna temple by buying for the devotees a 20-acre estate in Lechmoor Heath, 40 miles from London. It is an Elizabethan mansion surrounded by spectacularly lush and peaceful grounds, orchards, gardens, trees from all over the world, lakes, and meadows. This became Bhaktivedanta Manor, and devotees either visited or resided there, and those who lived there prepared vegetarian meals for Sunday gatherings that were open to outsiders as well as the London devotees. The Sunday feasts (often Harrison was on hand) included group chantings, discussions for the curious who were interested in Krishna, and dancing. Over the past years Harrison has turned much concert and recording money over to the temple, and paid for the publication of a lavishly printed religious text called *KRSNA: The Supreme Personality of Godhead,* by Prabhupada, who is part of the unbroken chain of succession reaching back to Lord Krishna himself; five thousand years ago Krishna appeared in his original transcendental form and spoke the *Bhagavad-Gita* (Song of God), which today remains the most important record of Krishna's words, and a classic source of Hindu philosophy with which Harrison is familiar.

In spite of the calm and strength he was getting from his spiritual involvements, Harrison's next professional challenge demanded more than usual from him, and in the months before and during his sessions for *All Things Must Pass,* George was understandably edgy and somewhat anxious about the project. This was an audacious step for him, though one he had helped prepare for by gaining broad experience as a producer and by being familiar with a broad range of studio players' styles and personalities. And he had the help of Phil Spector, who had also co-produced the *Layla* album.

The long-awaited triple record set (two sides of jams with the musicians on the record) hit record stores the last month of 1970, and immediately confirmed Harrison's enormous gifts as lyricist, musician, composer, and producer. He had achieved on the LP a fusion of instrumental elegance and thematic cohesiveness that has rarely been surpassed in rock music. The LP shined like a weighty gem, big and rich

and sparklingly bold, and it was the country's top-selling album for 7 weeks in a row. "I was really a bit paranoid," Harrison told Glazer of *Crawdaddy*. "There was a lot of negativism going down. I felt that whatever happened to my solo album, whether it was a flop or a success, I was going on my own just to have a bit of peace of mind. For me to do my own album after that—it was joyous. Dream of dreams.

"Even before I started the album I knew I was going to make a good album because I had so many songs, so much energy."

Once the rush of his great success took hold of him, Harrison resumed his studio career working alongside Ringo, Lomax again, Preston, David Bromberg, and Harry Nilsson, and producing a live concert by Ravi Shankar, Rakha, and Khan. Then he took the stage for a live rendition of "Badge" with Clapton, for his *Rainbow Concert* LP.

The live three-record set, *The Concert for Bangla Desh,* was released at the end of 1971, four months after the tumultuously acclaimed concert Harrison had put together in four weeks. There were bitter delays over the release of the LP due to squabbling over distribution and marketing. The financial mastermind (to use a *New York Times* description) behind the merchandising of the LP was Allen Klein, the Beatles manager. Klein's insistence on strict marketing stipulations was deliberately intended, he said, "to maximize the money for the charity and to preserve the artists' integrity." He was trying to keep the

retail price of the package down to around $9, although it was running for as high as $13 to $18 in some locales, with markups for middlemen and retailers. The *New York Times* speculated, through record industry interviews, that the dispute over release of the LP was tied to a feeling at Capitol and Columbia, which had signed distribution of the record and tape, that it would interfere with the Christmas season releases of their own major artists. Under agreements signed by Capitol for the record, the charity UNICEF would receive $5 royalty per LP, many times higher than is usual for artists in general, and Klein received a hefty advance from Capitol of $3.75 million. Harrison was so incensed by the bickering that on a rare talk show appearance, he angrily said to Dick Cavett, "You can create the money; then the problem is who to give it to. The album should have been out a month ago." But once it was out, and selling, more than 3 million were sold, raising well over $15 million, when ticket grosses and the concert film box-office figures were added. But even then, another major problem still had to be resolved with the Internal Revenue Service, which locked the money up for years until it could be decided how much would be given up, and how much would be taxed.

Through this, Harrison continued to play with other musicians like Bobby Keys and Ringo; joined John Lennon for a rare dobro solo on Lennon's "Crippled Inside" single (perhaps influenced by Clapton or Duane Allman, both of whom were interested in the dobro, a hillbilly-type slide instrument); produced another Shankar concert LP in the fall of 1972; and cut, in the first third of 1973, his own follow-up to *All Things Must Pass,* the enigmatic *Living in the Material World.*

The album was commercially potent, charted at number one in *Billboard* for 5 weeks. But while the LP has, in places, an even sharper production than *All Things* and contains some delightful musical structures, its lyrical context is less ingratiating. The sound has been pared down from *All Things*—gone is Spector's grandiose Wall of Sound (which worked well on some of the cuts)—but the words, in places, smack of a spiritual separatism that may have left

Harrison fans in the secular dust.

Here, Harrison bluntly repudiates his past successes and those who helped make them—the other fab three, notably—and sings, ''I only ask that what I feel should not be denied me now.'' There is his ingeniously biting satire ''Sue Me Sue You Blues,'' a pulsing-good rocker, and a lovely ballad that builds to a glorious, majestic peak, ''The Day the Earth Gets Round,'' but in which Harrison points out to the Lord, ''There are but a few who bow before you.'' Harrison, we are to presume, is among them, and the LP goes on like that, setting him off from the rest of his group in the past, and from all those who deny him his change of heart.

Above all, the LP raises the issue of

Living in the material world. Courtesy of Apple Records (Ken Marcus)

living in, but not necessarily of, the material world, and yet it doesn't fully distinguish the two. But Harrison, clearly, is trying to say they are different. A photograph on the inner sleeve shows him very much in the material world, at a sumptuous feast in his sprawling manor, surrounded by musician friends, drinking wine and eating bread and fruits and so on. A limousine awaits Harrison in the background on the circular driveway passing before his estate. When he has to "get back out of the material world," as he sings in the title track, it is suggested visually that he will go by limo. He warns of attachments to the material, transitory world of physical realities, yet he is immersed in them, and it isn't clear how he has resolved his own spiritualism with fabulous material wealth. The LP invited either cynicism among those who believe spiritualism implies asceticism, or cries of hypocrisy among those who believe Krishna consciousness is an elitist privilege—like certain ingenious tax loopholes—that are apparent only to people who attain an income high enough to require them. Both beliefs are obviously incorrect and rooted in ignorance, but the LP offered insufficient exposition of where Harrison stood between the material and the spiritual realism of his life, and so it marked the beginning of a troublesome three-year decline in his career and a period of personal tribulations. One thing was certain: the material world rewarded Harrison with a million-selling LP, and a hit, "Give Me Love," that was a top-ten smash for 6 weeks in a row.

Rex Features. Ravi Shankar and host

Unlike his more spiritual and philosophical pieces, Harrison's inspiring and affecting love songs from this period could not have been wholly autobiographical. His marriage had begun to unwind sometime in late 1973, and by the summer of 1974 Patti and George had split after eight years of marriage. Harrison had converted the ballroom of his estate into a full recording studio, in order to stay at home instead of trekking to London each time he wanted to cut a track. But the change wasn't enough to keep the marriage going, and by the summer Patti was on her own. She began showing up at Eric Clapton's summer comeback tour in 1974, his first appearances in three years. He had gone into temporary retirement from music to rehabilitate his life after a heroin habit. When he returned to concerts again Patti was often with him, and by the end of the tour they were together constantly.

Clapton had been George's closest musician friend for years, particularly when George had felt most directionless and insecure, during the White Album period; at that time Clapton joined him in the studio to help him play "While My Guitar Gently Weeps," the first non-Beatle superstar to participate in one of their studio recordings, and was indirectly responsible for George's revived interest in the guitar, and in playing slide style, which had become his signature sound. But earlier in the year Eric had hinted in an interview published in *Rolling Stone* that Patti had been the mysterious unnamed woman on *Layla*: "The lyrics said it all," Clapton noted in the interview. "Tried to give you a little consolation/ When your old man had let you down. / Like a fool I fell in love with you/ You turned my whole world upside down." Clapton elaborated further: "She was just trying to get his attention, get him jealous, and so she used me, you see, and I fell madly in love with her. He'd been into transcendental meditation for so long and yet couldn't keep his wife. All she wanted was for him to say 'I love you' and all he was doing was meditating."

Harrison later looked back on the triangle and said, without bitterness: "Eric's been a close friend of mine for years. I would rather she was with him than with some dope. We both loved Eric and still do." Splitting up, he felt, "was the best thing for us to do, and we just should have done it much sooner. But I didn't have any problem with it, Eric had the problem. Every

time I'd go see him, he'd really be hung up about it and I was saying, 'Fuck it, man, don't be apologizing,' and he didn't believe me. I was saying 'I don't care.' " Patti and George were divorced in June, 1977.

Clapton's published remarks seemed to suggest to some that a reason for the Harrisons' split-up was abstinence, rooted in George's spiritual pursuits. Glazer sounded George out on the subject:

The point is to have a balance between inner life and the external. Again, with relationships it never works if one person is into it and the other isn't. It's difficult on both sides. Usually if a fellow is into smack his girlfriend has to leave him or get in on it herself. It's like that. In a way we all have desires. We must learn either to fulfill them or terminate them. If you can do that by being celibate and it's easy to handle, it's okay. You can lose certain desires you had when you were younger, but particularly with sex and drugs—you have to watch it: you can't go "oh well, I'll just have a bit and then I'll be fulfilled." It doesn't work that way. First you have a bit and then you want more and more.

Whether or not abstinence makes Harrison's heart grow fonder, he survived the domestic blues of summer

1974, and was strong enough to face the recording of his next LP, *Dark Horse*, which was also the name of the record label he had set up earlier that year, though his own recordings were still on the Apple label from a Beatles-era contract (and would remain so until 1976).

George had already produced an LP for Dark Horse by Shankar, an elaborate orchestral project involving dozens of Indian musicians and for which he also played guitars, harmonium and autoharp. Then he produced an LP for the group Splinter, and on it played 6- and 12-string guitars, electric guitars, harmonium, moog synthesizer, 8-string bass, percussion, jew's harp, and bass—using a variety of easily decipherable pseudonyms like Harri Georgeson, Jai Raj Harisein, and P. Roducer.

More important to him, though, was a developing relationship with a lean, dark-haired Mexican-born Los Angeles woman named Olivia Arias. Olivia worked for A&M Records in their merchandising department and then moved over to Dark Horse Records as a secretary (A&M was distributing the small label then). She and George had talked on the phone many times from London and L.A., but George, before

Bill Elliot and Bobby Purvee of Splinter

*Alvan Meyerowitz.
The Dark Horse
stage banner for
the 1974 tour*

*Peter C Borsari/
Camera 5.
Olivia Arias*

coming to the States for work, asked a friend to check her out. She checked out, and once they met, in the later summer or fall of 1974, they became nearly inseparable. It was a relationship, says one friend, they each expected would work, "just an intuition, a thing they felt for each other over the phone. It was almost mystical the way they felt it happening."

Dark Horse was recorded in the fall of 1974, and it coincided with Harrison's plans to go on tour for the first time since 1966. This was a bold step for George, considering the bitter memories of road life and its disorienting extremes. But the comparatively smooth success of the Bangla Desh concert had sparked an interest in live playing again, and it seemed the time was right. However, despite the mood of anticipation of this first major U.S. concert tour of a Beatle in eight years, the Dark Horse tour faltered almost the moment it left the gate. Harrison's voice was weak and coarse at times, and crowd reaction to the Eastern-Western fusion set, with a 16-piece Indian orchestra, ranged from fidgety to indifferent. There were empty seats, and occasional open tension flowed between stage and crowd. George, for one thing, was committing lyrical heresy by changing one verse in the Beatles classic, "In My Life," from "I love you more" to "I love Him more." Secondly, crowds wanted some of the good rocking songs George had produced on his own, and instead found the tone of some early shows flat and diffuse.

Even at the tour's concluding show at Madison Square Garden, a writer for the *New Yorker* wrote "moments of real gladness were few . . . and the evening was filled with dissonances, contradictions, shortfalls." At show after show Harrison urged the crowds to chant Hare Krishna, or Christ-Christ, or Allah-Allah, and at least once, launched into a sermonette: "If we can all do it for thirty seconds without any hangups we'll blow the ceiling off this place." Moments later, the *New Yorker* observed, the chanting died down, and he exhorted the audience: "I'd just like to tell you that the Lord is in your hearts. I'm not up here jumping like a looney for my own

*Opposite:
Alvan Meyerowitz.
The 1974 tour,
Cow Palace, San
Francisco*

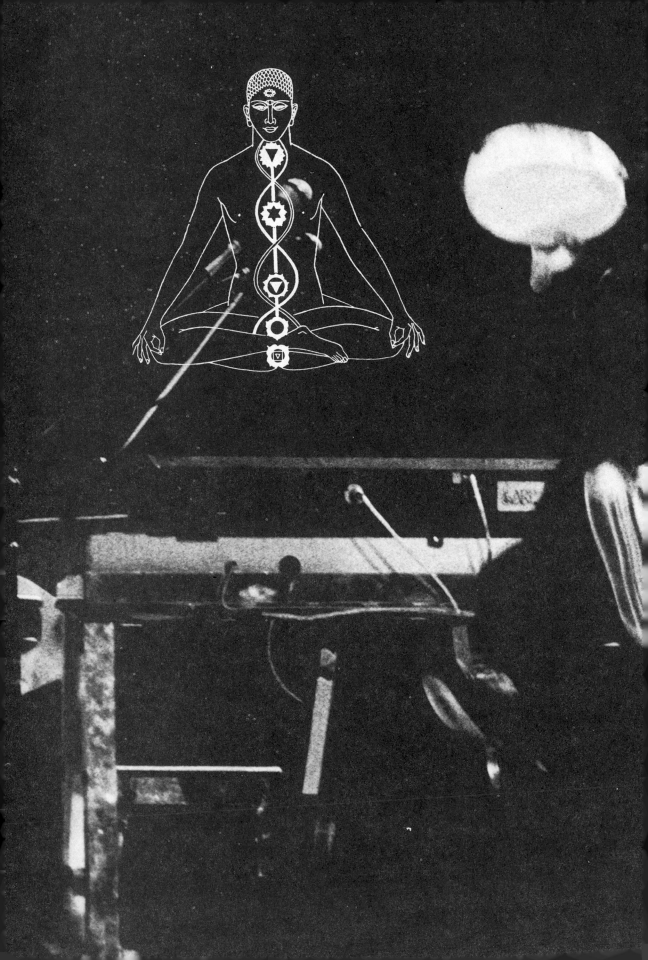

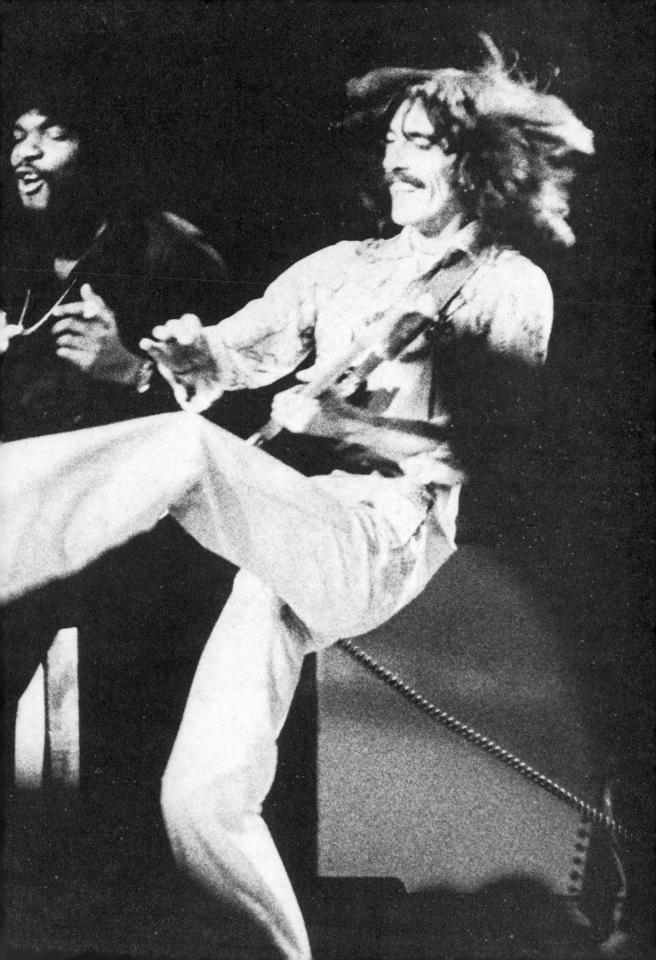

sake but to tell you that the Lord is in your hearts. Somebody's got to tell you. Let us reflect Him in each other."

In an article in *Rolling Stone* titled "Lumbering in the Material World," editor Ben Fong-Torres noted that one time Harrison took the microphone after a lukewarm response to a song and said, "I don't know how it feels down there, but from up here you seem pretty dead." Fong-Torres then reflected that Harrison's reluctance to do more Beatles material symbolized a "dismaying refusal to acknowledge his past and the fact that if he hadn't been a Beatle, he might not be doing a $4 million tour inside of seven weeks." (Harrison did designate the proceeds from several concerts for various medical charities.)

No one who had witnessed Harrison's press conference to kick off the tour, though, should have expected a show of gratitude. "I realize the Beatles did fill a space," he told reporters in Los Angeles, "in the 60s, and all the people the Beatles meant something to have grown up. It's like with anything. You grow up with it and you get attached to things. That's one of the problems in our lives, becoming attached to things, and it's appreciated that people still like them. But the problem comes when they want to live in the past and they want to hold onto something and are afraid to change." The LP, which did not come out until after the tour, had a song on it in which Harrison sings, "Ring out the old, ring in the new/ Ring out the false, ring in the true." Still, he stressed to Fong-Torres, "I know we get ten people who say the show sucks every night, and we get a hundred who when we we ask them did they like the show, say 'We got much more than we ever hoped for.'

"I don't care if nobody comes to see me, nobody ever buys another record of me. I don't give a shit, it doesn't matter to me, but I'm going to do what I feel within myself. Gandhi says create and preserve the image of your choice. The image of my choice is not Beatle George. But why live in the past? Be here now, and now, whether you like me or not, is where I am." Then he added, "Fuck it, my life belongs to me. It actually doesn't. It belongs to Him. My life belongs to the Lord Krishna and there's me dog collar to prove it. I'm just a dog and I'm led around by me dog collar by

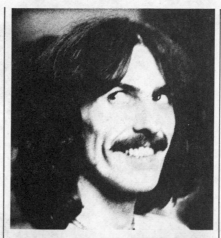

Krishna. I'm just the servant of the servant of the servant of the servant of the servant of Krishna. That's how I feel. Never been so humble in all my life, and I feel great."

Lighter moments helped carry the tour along, particularly when Harrison, Shankar, and Harrison's father stopped by the White House—at the invitation of Jack Ford, who had seen a concert in Utah. Harrison, dressed in furry red Tibetan boots, a plaid jacket, and orange pants, exchanged motto buttons with Ford—Harrison's OM for Ford's WIN (Whip Inflation Now). "He was much easier to meet than I would have expected," Harrison found. "He was not all that familiar with my music, but you can imagine the number of things he's got on his plate."

The LP was a relative flop for Harrison, perhaps a result of the disappointing reviews of tour performances. It stayed in the top ten for "only" 5 weeks, in early 1975. Then in May and June of that year he recorded his next LP, *Extra Texture—Read All About It,*

Ohnothimagen.
Courtesy of
Apple Records

Opposite:
Alvan Meyerowitz.
Billy Preston and
Ravi Shankar on the
1974 tour.

Previous page:
Joseph Sia.
Madison Square
Garden, 1975

and self-effacingly referred to himself in production credits as "OHNOT-HIMAGEN," which breaks down phonetically into "Oh not him again." Perhaps George was anticipating further hostile reception to his work. Indeed, a year later he would look back on that period and call it "depressing." Predictably, the lyrics of the LP reflect it, and the sound of the album indicates further dilution and dissipation of his once sharply focused and resolute skills in the studio. Where earlier works were lucidly assertive as on *All Things Must Pass*, there are moments on this LP

where the music degenerates into muddled messianism, and the overall tone of the LP is dark and troubling. The "let's carry on" optimism of *All Things* ("It's not always going to be this grey") had suddenly turned into titles like "World of Stone" and "Grey Cloudy Skies." There were no hits off the LP, and it marked the low point of his career, at least commercially. The LP reached only to number 8 on *Billboard,* and then *Extra Texture* was old news—out of the top 100—within two months of its release, the hastiest retreat of any of his LPs.

George spent the winter holiday season at home in England with Olivia, preferring the colder Christmas season to that of L.A.—but was back in the States two months later to give a benefit concert for the record—the public record that is. Harrison was in New York to defend himself in a plagiarism suit brought against him by Bright Tunes Publishing Company on behalf of the Chiffons, a black singing group whose early 1960s hit, "He's So Fine," was allegedly ripped off when Harrison wrote and recorded his own

hit, "My Sweet Lord," in 1970. There were lengthy hearings, six-foot-high charts of notes, "experts" brought in to explain the creative musical process, and the commonly derivative nature of inspiration in rock music. Harrison himself arrived one afternoon with his guitar and played out a bit of how he creates a song, confessing to the judge that he was a "jungle musician" who didn't know how to read music. But in September 1976, Judge Richard Owen ruled that Harrison had indeed committed a copyright infringement, though the Judge noted he did not believe Harrison had done it deliberately. "It is clear that 'My Sweet Lord' is the very same song as 'He's So Fine,' " he went on. "That is, under the law, copyright infringement, and is no less so though subconsciously accomplished." The judge felt Harrison "knew this combination of sounds would work because it already had worked in a song his conscious mind did not remember."

Months later Harrison confessed "My Sweet Lord" may have been a straight cop of an old tune, but not the

*Peter C Borsari/
Camera 5.
With Bob Marley
in Los Angeles,
and (opposite)
Olivia Arias*

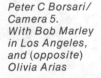

one for which he owed $400,000 in damages. Rather, he explained it was more directly inspired, in attitude as much as melodic structure, by the Edwin Hawkins Singers' "Oh Happy Day," a public domain tune. "I've written enough songs now so whatever they say, I'm cool. I know the motive behind writing the song and I don't feel guilty about it at all. If you could sing into a computer so it says 'You're okay,' or 'Sorry,' then I'd be willing because the last thing I want to do is spend my life in court. It made me so paranoid about writing that I thought I don't even want to touch this guitar. Somebody may own that note or this note."

He wasn't totally gun-shy, however,

Dark Horse LP for A&M distribution in July, after the termination of his long-term commitment to Apple and Capitol Records. But he was late now, and A&M was suing him for a whopping $10 million in damages to dissolve the deal along with Dark Horse Records, which included Shankar and groups like Jiva, Splinter, and Attitudes. The company claimed it had spent $2.6 million to launch the label, plus $1 million as an advance for Harrison, a sum Harrison was supposed to pay back if he didn't deliver the LP, the suit claimed. Then Harrison's attorney countercharged that the label owed *Harrison* $6.5 million, and that he would have signed with Capitol had he known A&M had incurred more than

Courtesy of Dark Horse Records/ Warner Bros (Bob Cato)

Wide World Photos. With Paul Simon on NBC's "Saturday Night" promoting "33⅓"

and turned out a late-1976 LP called *Thirty-Three and a Third,* which was received by critics and fans alike as Harrison's best work in several years— optimistic, musically buoyant, humorous and, most important, free of the didactic ramblings of his two previous LPs. But it wasn't an easy project, and Harrison had to get over a two-month bout with hepatitis and a dismaying recurrence of the Sue Me Sue You Blues before he could present it to the world.

The illness had caused a delay in the sessions and Harrison blew the deadline for the release, which A&M had planned for July. Under A&M's agreement with Harrison, signed in 1974, at the creation of Dark Horse, Harrison would record his first

half a million dollars in credit losses. Despite the murky legalese, it was also felt in some quarters that A&M suddenly wanted to bale out of the deal because it feared Harrison—and the lesser names—were simply not commercially potent any longer, and also because of "personal problems" between Harrison and some A&M executives.

The case was settled, and Harrison's label, and master tapes, were bought out by Warner Brothers Records. The ingratiating album, *Thirty-Three and a Third,* came out in late 1976 and was a huge relief for Harrison—as well as for fans and critics who had soured on his work for two or three years. There was a single hit off the LP, a sarcastically

humorous send-up of the plagiarism case ("This Song"), and the album sold three quarters of a million units.

Harrison was so glad to have his two lawsuits behind him that he agreed to go on a promotional tour to hype the LP—something he himself might have considered unimaginable, and unnecessary, five or ten years earlier. He, with Olivia, went around to five major cities with label president Mo Ostin, in the Warner jet plane, met the press, showed several riotously funny film clips done for the promo blitz (to go along with previewing "This Song" and another cut on the album, "Crackerbox Palace"), and probably did more interviews in two weeks than he had done in ten years. But he seemed relaxed, open, in excellent health. For instance, he and Olivia pulled up at the press luncheon set up in New York's swank Drake Hotel in a block-long white limousine, and when the two skinny vegetarians, T-shirted and jeaned, crouched out of the limo, and arrived at the luncheon, the horde of press converged around them and proceeded to move as one organism, like a giant centipede with a hundred feet, at every change of direction signalled by George. But he smiled freely—revealing his newly capped and straightened teeth—and despite the furrowed brow and cheeks, he spoke openly, without the tension or the Hari-er-than-thou smugness that characterized his 1974 tour. He made deliberate, sustained eye contact with people, seemed to enjoy the opportunity to talk to so many record industry people all at once, and, after explaining that the title of the LP referred to his age at the time it was recorded, seemed in full synch again with his career and his inner life. It was a fitting title. As an artist, George, at thirty-three and a third, was redeemed.

For much of his post-Beatle life, Harrison has shared his time between homes in Friar Park, in England, and in Beverly Hills. Until mid-1976 he owned a $700,000 mansion in Beverly Hills that had a guest house on the grounds, a tennis court, and a swimming pool painted black. When he and Olivia found that home too large, they sold it and bought a smaller, rustically elegant home, in Beverly Hills that assured them of privacy. Set far from the public road, it can't be seen by passersby. It is all-wood, has large stained-glass windows, and is peaceful and tastefully decorated.

When George and Olivia were between homes in 1976 and George had to be in Los Angeles to edit some film footage of his 1974 tour, they stayed in the house that Ringo Starr and his fiancee, Nancy Andrews, were then renting in Hollywood Hills. Ringo and Nancy were away at the time, but a friend of Harrison's who visited George and Olivia there recalled feeling George's impact on the place immediately upon entering through the door.

"There was a serene and calming presence that George and Olivia gave off. George had fresh flowers placed in the home and there was incense burning, pictures of holy men, the smell of curried rice dishes—long-grain rice—wafting in from the kitchen. They're both health food eaters. You know something is going on when they're around but it isn't something George shoves down your throat. They are both very thoughtful, and he has a great sense of humor. She is a lovely woman, far from that Hollywood-model type, far too spiritual. The harmony between them is clear and apparent to anyone around them, yet they don't perform sex in front of you on the floor. They are quite attentive to each other's needs and well-being and there is genuine caring going between them. It's quite lovely to see and it has a calming effect on people around them."

When they are in Los Angeles, which is usually several months a year, they are likely to spend time with the few close musician friends Harrison enjoys being around—including Clapton and Patti. They all get on socially both when Eric comes to L.A. to work and when they're in England, where Eric owns a home not far from George's.

Notwithstanding the unique situation of his promotional tour, Harrison remains strenuously press-shy, and harbors a still strong dread of publicity shaped by the media shell-shock of Beatlemania. He still makes occasional weeks-long trips to India to visit friends or to drop in on religious festivals, or to meet with some of the holy men who have helped shape his reli-

gious life, men like Sai Baba, India's celebrated Man of Miracles, or other gurus, yogis, and swamis.

On the unavoidable topic of a Beatles reunion Harrison has at times seemed to be the most willing, despite his strident denunciations of past glories of Beatlehood. He has said, perhaps felicitously, that he would do it "if someone were crazy enough to put up $50 million and the others were willing" (a reference to an L.A. fast-buck promoter who said he could reunite the Beatles for $50 million). Then again he has said, "The four of us are so tied up with our own lives and life goes so fast. It's not beyond the bounds of possibility, but we'd have to want to do it for the music's sake first."

Harrison is a Pisces—two fish swimming in opposite directions—and he has used that sign to explain the nature of dualisms, emanations, and his earnest search for a reality that goes beyond them all and encompasses God. "Yin-yang. Hot-cold. Yes-no. Black-white. Up-down. They all must exist, they both must exist, or they can't exist. How can you measure cold if you don't know hot? It's all part of the duality of the physical world. The world is a very serious place to live in and at the same time it's such a joke."

Another great duality in his life is that he is fond of saying that while the biggest break in his life was joining the Beatles, the biggest break since then was getting out of the Beatles. This dualism—the geometrically increasing wealth and fame and the growing inner despair over self-identity—propelled Harrison into his spiritual exploration: "It is one of our perennial problems, whether there is a God. From the Hindu point of view

each soul is divine. All religions are branches of one big tree. It doesn't matter what you call him as long as you call."

Harrison credits a variety of holy men with influencing his life, and he seeks some of them out when he goes to India or visits a Krishna temple in London or Los Angeles. He has said that the most influential figure was the yogi Paramahansa Yogananda, who "left his body in 1952" but whose writings George knows well. Descriptions of what God is are impossible by their very nature, since God goes beyond all descriptive specificity, but metaphors are often used to illustrate the relationship between maya-reality and God-reality: Yogananda's metaphor in his autobiography was simple and graphic: "Just as cinematic images appear to be real but are only combinations of light and shade, so is the universal variety a seeming delusion. The planetary spheres, with their countless forms of life, are naught but figures in a cosmic motion picture . . . . One's values are profoundly changed when he is finally convinced that creation is only a vast motion picture; and that not in, but beyond it, lies his own reality." He also wrote that for men, under the "mayan, or natural, law, the flow of life energy is toward the outward world; the currents are wasted and abused in the senses."

For Harrison, Krishna consciousness has been his path to Eternal Light, and in an introduction to the book *KRSNA, The Supreme Personality of Godhead,"* he wrote:

He has both the personal and impersonal aspects to his personality which is SUPREME, ETERNAL, BLISSFUL, and full of KNOWLEDGE. As a single drop of water has the same qualities as an ocean of water, so has our consciousness the qualities of GOD'S consciousness. . . . But through our identification and attachment with material energy (physical body, sense pleasures, material possessions, ego, etc.) our true TRANSCENDENTAL CONSCIOUSNESS has been polluted, and like a dirty mirror, is unable to reflect a pure image.

With many lives, our association with the TEMPORARY has grown. This impermanent body, a bag of bones and flesh, is mistaken for our true self, and we have accepted this temporary condition to be final.

If there's a God, I want to see him. It's pointless to believe in something without proof, and Krishna consciousness and meditation are methods where you can actually obtain God perception. You can actually see God and hear Him, play with Him. It might sound crazy, but he is actually there with you.

Harrison's conscientiously ambiguous love songs, aimed at woman-and-God, are a way of expressing his belief that the love of another is the same as love of self and love of God, that they are all elements of the same reality, as drops of water relate to the ocean. The love found in another is the love in all of us, he believes, and through its realization lies the reality beyond it, the path to God-love.

Clearly for George Harrison one of the problems about his spiritual growth is what the devotees in the Krishna temple might refer to as the "bad company" surrounding him in the record industry—people of low, or no, spiritual self-awareness. Harrison is not an actual devotee because he has never taken the four vows for Krishna initiation: no illicit sex, no intoxicants, including cigarettes, coffee, and tea; no gambling; and no meat. (Harrison is vegetarian, but smokes cigarettes and drinks.) But even among his Krishna brethren, his wealth poses no obstacle to pure Krishna enlightenment. "Limousine karma or tin-can karma—it's the same thing," says one devotee, who helped George record the London temple chants, and who visited him often at his home on Henley. "It's all a matter of how much you've understood. Renunciation doesn't mean giving up all your money. It means leaving the full enjoyment of material wealth, understanding the roots of that enjoyment and making the proper utilization of your wealth. It isn't that George Harrison is incapable of real spiritual consciousness simply because he is wealthy. As a master once said, 'Krishna is simple for the simple, difficult for the crooked. And George is basically a simple, unsophisticated person. When Prabhupada met him he called George "a nice boy." The problem for George is that the world he works in is too brutal for the flower of Krishna consciousness to grow in. His fame may be an impediment to him, but only because he may not be free to come and go to the temples and surround himself with other devotees.''

Harrison, in his candidly revealing interview with *Crawdaddy's* Glazer, admitted that rock and roll superstardom may be a ''deviation'' from what matters: ''Is it a priority to go around being a rock and roll star? There's no time to lose really. There are lots of times I've been heavily into it and then other times I come right back out of it. There are a lot of people in this business that I love, friends, who are really great but who don't have any desire for knowledge or realization. . . . It's good to boogie once in a while, but when you boogie all your life away, it's just a waste of a life and of what we've been given.''

Harrison elaborated on an interpretation of a painting included on the *Material World* LP package, taken from the *Bhagavad-Gita*. It shows Krishna and Arjuna in a chariot drawn by five horses over a battlefield. ''We are in these bodies,'' Harrison said, ''which is a kind of chariot. And we're going through this incarnation, this life, which is kind of a battlefield. The five senses of the body are the five horses pulling the chariot, and we have to get control over the chariot by getting control over the reins. And Arjuna in the end says, 'Please Krishna, you drive the chariot.' ''

Ten years earlier Harrison had been in a kind of chariot, racing all over the world with three friends in it. Their world was to them a kind of battlefield, but then there was no Krishna to hold the reins. Instead there was only Brian Epstein, limousine drivers, roadies and promoters, all pulling on the bits, sending the chariot off in a precarious, lurching pace. The dust over the first battlefield had settled; and the dust over the second, with Krishna guiding his spiritual chariot, has now settled, because Harrison himself is at peace with his own self-realization. He needn't prove it any longer to others, as he has proven it to himself. His story is one of the most paradoxical and enduring fables of popular culture—a sort of holy man-millionaire strapped to a Fender guitar, voicing the unforgettable sounds of a Beatle accent, but now describing the sweetly shivering deliverance of his soul unto Krishna:

Unless we bring along Christ or Krishna or Buddha or whatever guru, we can go so far on our own without divine guidance or without being established in some sort of God consciousness, then we are going to crash our chariots, turn over and get killed on the battlefield. That's why we say 'Hare Krishna Hare Krishna,' asking Krishna to come and take over the chariot. It's beautiful, you know, because it works.

Krishna & Arjuna.
(A C Bhaktivedanta Swami Prabhupada)

GENTLY WEEPING

4 As a guitarist, George Harrison has always conceded limits in his technical skills. Over the years scores of rock and roll guitarists have been faster players, more theatrical, more physically intense, more ambitious to explore the electronic gadgetry of the instrument. It would be unfair to measure his art, and impact, in those terms alone. Imagine, instead, the guitar to be a foreign language. Harrison, a student of this language, has developed a vocabulary placing him at an intermediate level of sophistication and breadth. When he speaks the language, though, his delivery is unerringly accurate, and while he may not dazzle native speakers by reciting lengthy passages from its finest literature, he reveals to the native an even subtler talent—his mastery of a complex syntax and elegant inflection that allows him to piece together simple but flawless sentences; ideas flow together with a minimum of effort, and with his efficient, intelligent use of the words and phrases he does know, Harrison can articulate his most intimate feelings, wishes, needs. Without a syllable of excess or an empty breath, Harrison speaks with eloquence and lucidity where his classmates too often turn to slang, profanities, or facile colloquialisms uttered reflexively.

The Beatles always realized that the sum of their gifts as musicians was dwarfed by the whole of their communal magic. It is inconceivable to imagine the Beatles plus another musician; it is likewise impossible to imagine any one of them missing, or for that matter, fitting in with a different band. Jimi Hendrix, Clapton, Jimmy Page, Keith Richard, or John McLaughlin—any of these guitar virtuosos would have fatally bent the Beatles out of shape with their guitar playing. Harrison's job was different: to help them sustain the balance that characterized their glorious six-year reign as the world's best group. Restraint was virtuous; power, playing for its own sake, could have been disastrous to them. They were a musical eco-system, dependent on each other for life-sustaining harmony and control. A deep shift in the nature of any one element in their chemical chain reactions would have mutated them and seriously altered, if not killed, the organism.

Nearly every other famous rock group of their day assumed the emotional character of its dominant ego (i.e., the Rolling Stones' Jagger, the Who's Roger Daltrey, Led Zeppelin's Robert Plant). But the Beatles' egos meshed so seamlessly that, though they seemed distinct in the mass eye, they were in fact thoroughly collectivized; and they became in the end not four separate conflicting egos but one vastly complex personality with four consistently discernible moods. Musically, this meant that all individual artistry existed for the good of the group; they were technically conservative and artistically Marxist. This explains Harrison's unfailing "tastefulness" as a player, his restraint, precision, and fluid lyricism. These were cardinal Beatle virtues. No long, roaring solos; no superfluous fills between verses simply to keep the fingers and strings hot; no puerile guitar-envy played out along the neck of the solid-body Fender. Harrison, alone among his peers, maintained a rigorously Platonic affair with his instrument— deep and beautiful, rooted in respect, never fixation. And, most wondrously, as a function of his unsurpassed celebrity as a Beatle guitarist, this companionship grew, matured, took on vital significance in his life—to the delight of hundreds of millions of well-wishers all over the planet.

Harrison's playing on the earliest Beatles releases is rudimentary, with numerous blatant borrowings from his idols, like Chuck Berry, Carl Perkins, Buddy Holly. there is a series of Carl Perkins-type rockabilly riffs on songs like "Honey Don't," "Act Naturally," "No Reply," "I'm a Loser," "I Don't Want to Spoil the Party." And among their early homages to black rock and roll songs of the late 50s were adaptations of "Roll Over Beethoven," "Boys," "Chains," "Dizzy Miss Lizzy," "Kansas City," "Long Tall Sally," and "Money (That's What I Want)." Harrison's lead lines were simple, brief, and, incredibly, almost always memorable. In songs like "I Should Have Known Better," "A Hard Day's Night," "Please Please Me," "Hold Me Tight," "Baby's in Black," "I'll Follow the Sun," "Every Little Thing," "What You're Doing," and "And I Love Her," among many

Opposite:
Michael Zagaris.

75

others, right up until the release of *Help!*, Harrison's lead structures were designed to enforce, not dilute, the melodic themes established by Lennon and McCartney. In "Eight Days a Week," or "Every Little Thing," he virtually echoes the melody with a guitar voicing by working his own lead into a rich chord structure shifting beneath the top melodic line. Indeed, in the early Beatles works, Harrison's notion of lead guitar comes closer to what a 70s rhythm guitarist provides a rock band of today, rather than the freely independent lead solo that has little connection to the tune except the basic chord pattern, and whose main purpose seems to be to showcase the sheer physical intensity of the guitarist with what is referred to somewhat derogatorily as "power-riffing." While more contemporary guitarists have defined the lead guitar essentially as a weapon of maximal rock and roll power, Harrison always allowed his minimal art to flourish humbly in the midst of the greatest compositions of his day.

In the period of *Rubber Soul, Revolver,* and *"Yesterday". . . and Today* (a package of unreleased or single records)—fall 1965 through spring 1966—Harrison was first exposed to the sitar, and experienced his first bout with touring-blues. He was examining not only the Beatle phenomenon and its role in the cosmos, but was also looking at new time signatures and the eerie Indian scale as it sounds on the sitar. It's on these albums, of course, that we first hear the sitar used, on "Norwegian Wood," as well as a different, more jangly voicing of acoustic guitar chords on "I'm Only Sleeping," and "Here, There and Everywhere." There is an extended and jaunty sitar solo through-out "Love You Too," as well as a number of rich and driving electric gui-tar chord-runs on "And Your Bird Can Sing," one of his most distinct pieces, not to mention the gritty note-bending fills on "She Said She Said." As recording techniques improved, Harrison's playing—and the sounds he created—became more polished and clear.

After his two-month trip to India at the conclusion of the 1966 summer tour, Harrison returned with new and profound insights into the guitar and, of course, himself. His contribution to *Sgt. Pepper,* "Within You Without

Rex Features.

You," is texturally exquisite, and his droning vocal syllabication—evenly spaced single syllables—balances the resonant pulsings from deep within the tabla. And when the sitar breaks off into its fluttering solo—shattering the 4/4 time-signature frame of most rock and roll, it is as if Harrison has penetrated a musical "wall of illusion" as well, and has been struck by a wholly new artistic vision about rhythms and their possibilities.

Sgt. Pepper also bears a much more forceful rock sound than the Beatles had achieved before, as in the opening title track, kicked off by George's four-note lead-in. Also, he adds soaring single-note fills in "Good Morning, Good Morning," not overbearingly, but innovatively all the same. And on songs like "Fixin' a Hole" and "With a Little Help from My Friends," he provides near constant backing with chord-playing rather than single notes, again, a reiteration of his unique function as a lead player. A lot of subtle studio gimmicks and tricks appeared on the tapes—perhaps interpreted in 1967 as an invitation to consciousness-altering, or sense-expanding drugs. But, too, this was a reflection of the Beatles' holiday in the studio, when they had time to work on an LP without the pressures of road life. And so they manipulated the machinery of the studio to best advantage. And in the process, Harrison was coming across new possibilities, new sounds for his guitar.

The White Album was recorded amid strong outward-pulling forces. Two Beatles left sessions briefly, Eric Clapton came in to give George support—musically and emotionally—for his "Gently Weeps." Harrison's tightening embrace of Krishna consciousness was weakening the Beatles' hold on him. The album reflects Harrison's urge to break loose and explore his own artistry, and to work with the talents of other musicians.

There is a more tenderly resonant use of acoustic guitars on this LP, as on "Little Piggies," and (though not on the LP, of this period), "Here Comes the Sun" and "Hey Jude." Harrison plays a rare finger-picking lead on "Dear Prudence," a deeply affecting descending run with alternating bass notes (likely he lowered the E bass-note to D to give a more resonant "open tuning" effect in the key of D); he also plays rough rock and roll,

achieving a more metallic (as in heavy metal) sound on cuts like "Revolution" and "Helter Skelter." His solo on the latter is a brilliant display of economy of phrasing and subtlety. The song opens with a flame-throwing fury— some 60 slashes at the guitar fitted into three chord changes, as McCartney's voice builds to its hysterical pitch, at which point both dissolve into the thunderously heavy rhythm section powered by an uncommonly *big* beat from Ringo and a deep, *deep* bass line. The solo is just 11 or 12 notes long, introduced by a major guitar chord struck twice, like a colon in a sentence: the notes seem to slither around the structures of the chords, descending gradually, then rising and falling again, hooking up, then falling to rest. It is an exhilarating rock phrase, powerful and sleek.

Then, on *Abbey Road,* Harrison plays some equally hard rock riffs, particularly on the "She's So Heavy" drone, again on "Polythene Pam," and "She Came in through the Bathroom Window," and most noticeably in the ascending volley of power-chord sequences in "The End," probably the longest uninterrupted guitar instrumental they ever recorded.

And yet this LP, along with "Gently Weeps," signals Harrison's growth in another direction, toward the sweet, lyrical solo, moving and evocative. The looping slide guitar solo that would become his signature riff had started taking shape with "While My Guitar Gently Weeps," on the White Album, which Clapton also played lead on, and worked his way into his beautifully fluid solo on "Something," from *Abbey Road.* A new flexibility and self-expression became evident here, and it all came together on his first solo project, *All Things Must Pass.*

The range and execution of the material on the *All Things* album is extraordinary. On "Wah-Wah," set in major chords, the rock is driving and hard, with horns popping in for fills between George's bobbing, teasing slide guitar. On "Isn't It a Pity," the slow-moving minor-chord sequence suggests a futile, melancholic mood of pain and hurting ("how we break each other's hearts and cause each other pain"). The song shows George's great capacity to squeeze feeling from a note, to extend and sustain it for just the right time, and to use space as a positive factor in phrasing between lyrics and instrumental arrangements. At all costs he avoids clutter and glut, two evils of overproduction that scar so many other rock self-producers. (Spector did push the LP in the direction of his lavish overdubbings, but never at the expense of George's guitar statements, only as rhythmic tide behind the vocal and guitar tracks.)

The twin-lead guitar structures, which Dickey Betts and Duane Allman were also developing into a distinct and recognizable style in the South, comes to life for the first time on this LP. It creates a wistful, weary feeling of loss, or of life's bittersweetness. Harrison's guitar seems to sigh with the notes as they peak, then roll down and swoop low before soaring again, like a pair of gulls cruising over a bay at sunset, in an effortless glide carried by the wind. He achieves this effect on the solo in "I'd Have You Anytime," and "What Is Life." Harrison's slide technique is neither as bluesy nor as blazingly fast as many others, but his good taste is unexcelled. And yet on "Apple Scruffs," he strums muscularly all by himself (with a harmonica) to evoke the chilly, lonely winter days in London when his fans would wait outside the office windows of Apple Records to catch a glimpse of a hero. The touching and moving song is about the fans' lonely waiting, and yet it could be about Harrison's wait to be out on his own, "through the pleasure and the pain, in the fog and the rain."

Harrison's next studio LP, *Living in the Material World,* confirmed his stature in the material world among great studio players (of whom he used Clapton; Bobby Whitlock; Gary Wright; and Pete Drake, the Nashville superproducer and pedal-steel wizard). With this album Harrison shows he can really play the dobro, the metallically resonant hillbilly instrument played like a slide guitar (on "Sue Me Sue You Blues"); he strums ringing harmonics on "The Day the World Gets Round"; and he brings his twin-guitar lead style to new levels of expressiveness on his hit single, "Give Me Love." The music on this LP is every bit as solid and inventive as on the previous one, and at times the production is appealingly sharper, his playing reflecting great clarity.

Harrison's guitar playing became, like some of his compositions, diluted and diffused over the next two LPs, and there are few standout moments on either *Dark Horse* or *Extra Texture.* Many of the tunes lack the lucid focus of earlier works, and they're quirkier, less gripping emotionally as his lyrics tend to become more didactic and, at times, depressing (as on "Grey Cloudy Skies" and "World of Stone" from *Extra Texture*). It was at this time that Harrison was splitting with his wife; and his 1974 tour was anything but triumphant. This shows.

But with the burden of two lawsuits lifted in 1976, he seemed to regain his sense of humor on his *Thirty-three and a Third* LP. It struck a refreshing balance between his spiritual needs in music (heard in the prayerful "Dear One," dedicated to a yogi he respected, and in the sermonette "See Yourself") and the secular/humorous side of his life (as in "This Tune," the satire of his plagiarism case, and "Crackerbox Palace" (an ingeniously funny rock version of Cole Porter's "True Love"). "This Song" is vibrantly contemporary, with clear studio production and superb backup by Tom Scott on horns, Willie Weeks on bass, Billy Preston and Gary Wright on keyboards, and Alvin Taylor on drums. And Harrison's guitar plays sweet as ever in his slide-guitar riffs for "Crackerbox Palace." The LP's overall tone is laissez-faire, not righteous judgment; as Harrison sings, "It's What You Value." After two noncommercial, unfocused LPs and a troubling, disappointing, sometimes misguided national tour, Harrison seems once again to value most his ability to compose and play fine music that can reach his audiences.

What has set George Harrison apart from most every other guitarist of his generation is that he never confuses eloquence with technique. While many rock guitarists play numbingly repetitive licks in flagrant compensation for a lack of expressiveness, Harrison's approach has been almost the reverse: he has consistently turned to an ever-deepening lyrical fluency as a compensation for his openly acknowledged technical shortcomings. He has never taken that easy way out, and he has also played more single memorable lines of guitar music (the lead structures to "Day Tripper," "Ticket to Ride," "A Hard Day's Night," "My Sweet Lord," "Give Me Love," "Within You Without You," "In My Life,"—the list seems endless) than any other guitar player of his day.

IN GEORGE'S WORDS

5 The evolution of George Harrison's guitar playing is dramatic enough, but still more formidable is the change that has taken place in his lyricism—from his first Beatle writings, through the *Sgt. Pepper* period, and then onward as a solo artist. His earliest Beatle creations, like "Don't Bother Me" and "Taxman," give little hint of the changes that were to explode. "Don't Bother Me" is a simple little rocker written while George was cooped up sick in a hotel room somewhere. And the song, correspondingly, is mundane, cranky, aloof-sounding. "Taxman," which foretold the 70s parade of millionaire tax-exiles from the U.K.'s stranglehold to tax havens in the States, was a sardonic commentary on the Beatles' Sisyphean struggle against the Treasury: not only was the taxman taking nineteen parts for every one left the Beatles, but, sang Harrison,

If you drive a car, I'll tax the streets
If you try to sit, I'll tax your seat
If you get too cold I'll tax the heat
If you take a walk I'll tax your feet.

Harrison's humor was always clever, dry, and biting.

George's following Beatles songs were domestically rooted love songs, cries of loving and leaving. "You Like Me Too Much" is a half-serious and ironic bluff-calling:

You'll never leave me and you know
    it's true
'Cause you like me too much and I
    like you.

Then, in the bridge, Harrison softens, admits his own susceptibility:

If you leave me
I will follow you and bring you back
    where you belong.
'Cause I couldn't really stand it,
I admit that I was wrong.

While lyrics like these may unwittingly justify Harrison's chronic insecurity about writing in the presence of Lennon and McCartney—a David with *two* Goliaths to cope with—his melodies were every bit as tunefully breezy and mature, never lapsing into the platitudes of three-chord rock. And his casual intelligence was certainly above standard for his day.

One album later (*Help!*) Harrison's "I Need You" places *him* in the passive hot-spot. Now he likes *her* too much:

You don't realize how much I need
    you,
Love you all the time and never
    leave you.
Please come on back to me
I'm lonely as can be
I need you.

The song is a plea for reconsideration, the Quiet One hoping to patch things up. Then, on the psychic flip side, in "Think for Yourself," he takes a harder line: "Think for yourself, 'cause I won't be there with you," he warns; it's a hawkish laissez-faire tone: Dream on, he says

About the good things we can have
    if we close our eyes.
Do what you want to do
And go where you're going to

Now he's in the driver's seat.

On "Love You Too," from *Revolver,* a clear shift in mood is apparent. We become aware of his sitar-fixation of the period (the instrument solos sinuously throughout the piece), as well as a dead-serious concern about his own mortality, the passing of time, and the fleeting nature of wealth and fame— concerns he was just beginning to wrestle with. The Beatles were planning to end their touring career, and get back to the studio work they felt they had to leave behind so often. Perhaps too, Harrison, who was only 15 when he joined the band, was feeling his life slipping through his hands without a veto power over any of it:

Each day just goes so fast
I turn around it's past

Then he was also singing about his intensifying disillusionment with fame:

A lifetime is so short
A new one can't be bought

Now that he had achieved all the material comforts imaginable at that time, he was beginning to turn away from the material realm and look beyond it for deeper, lasting personal meaning. At the saturation point in monetary gratification, the first cracks in a wall of illusion made themselves lyrically visible in this song.

On the same album Harrison's head is "filled with things to say," in "I

*Opposite:
Joseph Sia*

Want to Tell You,'' but when he gets near his lover, ''the games begin to drag me down.'' One verse later, he admits a sort of existential pang of confusion: ''I feel hung up but I don't know why.'' And then, at the end of ''I Want to Tell You,'' there's a humorous allusion to the difference between the self and the socially determined ''mind'' that controls it, often with mutually antagonistic purposes:

If I'm unkind
It's only me, it's not my mind
That is confusing things.

Harrison raises the question of a conflict between instinct and reason, which, he may feel, reflects his growing awareness of a difference between the laws of maya (the real, physical world) and the divine law that governs through loving self-realization.

This song, which ends with an Indian-scale chant, quivering through a long-sustained major chord, prefigures the spirituality and exotic textures of ''Within You Without You.'' Again, the urgency theme is repeated: ''Never glimpse the truth, then it's far too late,'' and an earnest but righteous conviction about changing: ''Try to realize it's all within yourself / No one else can make you change.'' If we all do that, he hopes, ''the love we could all share'' might reach full realization.

If George's guitar gently wept on the White Album, his voice fairly raged—with self-doubt and, worse, self-laceration, over his disillusionment as the Beatles' world appeared to detain him from a spiritual audience with God. In ''Gently Weeps,'' he seems to tell himself—using the second person—that he doesn't know how "you were converted, you were perverted too" or that "no one alerted you." He looks around, sees the world is still turning, and his guitar gently weeps. Harrison is singing from outer space here: he sees nothing has changed; his impact on the things that matter is nil; he hasn't relieved anyone's suffering; he feels profoundly purposeless and cosmically irrelevant.

His Beatle attacks continue in this period with his lighter though no less revealing "Only a Northern Song" (the Beatles publishing company was Northern Song) from *Yellow Submarine*.

It doesn't really matter
What chords I play
Or words I say
Or time of day it is
'Cause it's only a Northern Song.

He also says that if their harmonies—vocal and, by extension, interpersonal—seem dark and dissonant, "You're correct, there's nobody there." Such nihilism directed at Harrison's past, and at external worldliness, is offset by the gushing inner bliss he expresses in a single included on the same LP, "It's All Too Much."

When I look into your eyes
You're always there for me
And the more I go inside
The more there is to see.

This song is the first Harrison composition using an ambiguous second person—divine, or female?—which pervades much of his work since 1969. Asked in an interview to resolve this ambiguity, Harrison smiled and said, "I like that. Singing to the Lord or to an individual is, in a sense, the same. I've done that consciously in some songs." At the song's finale, a celebratory explosion of heavy rock rhythms alternating between the two dominant major chords, Harrison exclaims his full joy before a blinding rush of spiritual love enveloping everything:

It's all too much for me to see
The love that's shining all around
  me.

Another song written in 1967 but recorded and released as a little-known single titled "The Inner Light," extends this notion of God-as-love and physical-world-as-illusion. The piece was recorded by Indian musicians in Bombay while George was there to visit the Maharishi's ashram. It has, like "Within You" and "Love You Too," an exotic Indian instrumentation.

Without going out of my door
I can know all things on earth
Without looking out my windows
I could know the ways of Heaven.

Here, inner light is the eternal light of God-consciousness; outer light, illuminating only the physical, temporary realm, is useless in finding Godliness; it's a trap, an optical illusion.

The farther one travels
The less one knows
Arrive without traveling
See all without looking.

From this point on, his writing is wrapped around one essential theme: sight and light, the treachery of physiological eyesight without true inner vision. His two most affecting songs from this period, his sweetest compositions, elaborate this theme: "Here Comes the Sun" uses the source of all physical light as a metaphor to celebrate his spiritual springtime:

Little darlin' it's been
A long cold lonely winter
Little darlin' it feels like years
Since it's been here
Here comes the sun.

In "Something," one of his most poignant compositions, Harrison is bewildered, overcome: "Something in the way she moves, attracts me like no other love." This love—again, perhaps ambiguous, ultimately—has been elevated from the fretfully possessive love of "You Like Me Too Much" to a total, self-assured, free love, undemanding and unconditional. The *Abbey Road* sessions were the Beatles' last, and for Harrison, his contributions to the LP fed the momentum he was gaining for his epochal solo take-off.

The *All Things Must Pass* album cover set the tone of the six-sided LP, and it visually severed any associations with the Beatles. Harrison is lean and scruffy, with a long beard and stringy hair past his shoulders. He is a weary solitary figure on a stool in his backyard garden, surrounded by reclining statues of grinning gnomes who mock the mood of the afternoon—grey, chilly, a colorless still-life. Harrison is solemn and gaunt, like someone who has just returned from burying a

85

beloved relative who has died after a long illness: sadness and loss, felt more with relief than with shock.

The Beatles' hilarity, self-parody, the pardonable smugness, their vision of the world through kaleidoscope eyeglasses—it's all light years behind him now. The "Art of Dying," he sings, is the best way to live—and love. We only have our physical bodies at "death"—and then we are "brought back by our desires to be a perfect entity . . ." Hardly standard rock and roll verse, but Harrison is singing in earnest now. He is repentant, he has wasted a lot of time, and he is sorry he didn't realize it all a long time ago. But he isn't self-pitying. He is cleansed of conflicts over his Fab Four karma. "It's not always going to be this grey," he promises, in the tenebrous but still positive title track, which moves slowly like a massive storm cloud passing before a late evening sun, dense and chilling in the middle, but glowing all around the edges with the warm flushes of hope from the sunset. And, as he did at the Bangla Desh concerts, he warns, "Beware of maya."

Images of vision abound throughout the album: "All I have is yours, all you see is mine," he sings, in "I'd Have You Anytime"; "I really want to see you," he prays, in "My Sweet Lord"; in "Isn't It A Pity" he sings, "Not too many people can see we're all the same/ And because of all their tears their eyes can't hope to see." And in the haunting "Beware of Darkness," he offers up a scary image of the "unconscious sufferer" wandering aimlessly down sidewalks.

Harrison's next LP, *Living in the Material World,* was musically tight and well crafted, with highly inventive textures and melodies, as in his tender "Give Me Love" and the thumping rockers like "Living in the Material World" and "Sue Me Sue You Blues." But as a lyrical work, the LP went beyond the simple, declarative goals of *All Things* and seemed, in places, to be Harrison's attempt at proving his spirituality—or at least litigating it in verse. The title track is a humorous but disparagingly hindsightful account of how he met the other three Beatles and "got caught up in the material world." Understatement Number Nine. Number Nine. But now he isn't staying around; he's got work to do in the material world, and then it'll be time to "get back out" of it:

I hope I would get out of this place
By Sri Lord Krishna's grace
My salvation from the material
    world.

If Harrison seems to be a defendant in the trial of his own soul, he expresses it, cleverly, by shifting the burden of proof to the scene of the Beatles' breakup. In "Sue Me Sue You Blues":

It's affidavit serving time
Sign on the dotted line
Hold your Bible in your hand
Now all that's left
Is to find yourself a new band.

The album sleeve photo shows Harrison not *cautious* of maya but immersed in maya, with a limo (to take him back out of the material world, presumably) waiting behind him. He's on his lawn (the sun has come out since *All Things Must Pass*) and enjoying a feast with some musician friends. He's toasting a glass of wine and wearing an OM button, which is his backstage pass to God's dressing room. And on the LP he's singing

I can see quite clearly now
Through those past years
. . . I only ask, that what I feel
Should not be denied me now
And it's been earned
And I have seen my life
Belongs to me
My love belongs to who can see it.

Courtesy of Apple Records

86

This is a challenge to go beyond appearances, beyond the photo he's given us. It's a metaphysical dare, a plea to trust him, requiring a leap of faith. And yet Harrison's plea is almost too strong, too confessional, as is the photo baiting us to fall for "the old maya routine"; it's as if he were saying, *See, you think a limo is more a part of the physical world than a bicycle is, but you're wrong. See, I can have me limos and still find true holy peace. You don't have to be poor to be spiritual and I can have it both ways.* And Lord knows, Krishna consciousness in no way excludes wealth; it has little to do with it, unless it's one's attachments to it that matter. Yet we get no explanation of this side of the coin. Harrison has warned about the optical illusions of maya—and here he has created one, is generating cynicism that may have kept his audience from the full enjoyment of his still very fine music. The LP began a decline in his musical vitality and commercial impact that lasted through most of 1976, when he released *Thirty-Three and a Third*.

Harrison's next two LPs, *Dark Horse* and *Extra Texture: Read All About It*, in 1974 and 1975 respectively, have some fine musical moments, but are, in the larger picture, pale and negative, and lyrically more flaccid and indulgent than the previous two.

Even his humor, as on the "Bye Bye Love" parody, has turned somewhat acidic, and the sound of the cut is pained and morose—perhaps because his wife had split and run off with Clapton:

There goes our lady
With a "you know who"
I hope she's happy
And Clapper too.

There is a Spector-esque cut, "Ding Dong Ding Dong," which repeats in rather silly cheerleading fashion:

Yesterday today was tomorrow
And tomorrow today will be
    yesterday
Ring out the false
Ring in the true
Ring out the old
Ring in the new.

Not his most sophisticated lyrical effort.

The title track describes George as a "dark horse, running on a dark course," and by this time he seems to be limping a bit as well. The glittering positivism and sureness has now degenerated into metaphysical qualms, depression, loneliness. If Harrison is referring to the Beatles here, in "Simply Shady," the image is striking, filled with doubts and fears:

No sooner had I sown it
When I began to reap.
I was torn from shallow water
And plunged into the deep
And as I started drowning
I clung onto a straw
That somehow kept me floating
While my madness craved for more.

And in "So Sad," a searingly beautiful song with gorgeous slide-guitar riffs:

The winter has come to eclipse out
    the sun
That has lighted my love for some
    time
And a cold wind now blows
Not much tenderness flows
From the heart of someone feeling
    so tired
And he feels so alone with no love
    of his own

And "Maya Love," he says, is "like the sea flowing in and out of me"; it isn't so easy now to "get back out of it."

But there are also two prayerful songs, one, "Far East Man," which seems to be about a holy man:

Looks like right here on earth
God, it's hellish at times
But I feel that a Heaven's in sight
And I can't let him down.
Got to do what I can
I can't let him drown
He's a Far East man.

It is as if by thinking of his *savior's* drowning, Harrison is better able to cope with his own, a method that makes identification with a spiritual figure easier, perhaps. Harrison reached for the straw that saved him from drowning, and now in his hour of doubt, he offers *himself* as that straw, fusing himself with an image of his own salvation, in an act of surrender. And the LP concludes with a jaunty chant to Jai Sri Krishna:

He whose sweetness flows
To any one of those
That cares to look His way
See His smile
Jai sri radhe jai krishna.

Extra Texture is Harrison's weakest LP, musically and lyrically, one he himself referred to as "depressing." And he's right. The images of light and sun are forcefully reversed here, and in "Grey Cloudy Skies" (they weren't always going to be this grey, remember?), doubt and fear have turned to despair:

Now I only want to be with no pistol
    at my brain
But at times it gets so lonely
Could go insane
Could lose my brain
Now I only want to live with no tear-
    drops in my eyes
But at times it feels like no chance
No clear blue skies.

And in "World of Stone" he has retreated from his once near-missionary zeal to singing:

Wise men you won't be
To follow the like of me.

And later:

Such a long way to go
Such a long way from home
In this world made of stone.

Harrison's two songs of love on the LP are quirky, and lyrically almost mockingly juvenile. In "You" he sings:

I, I love, love
N' I n' I love you.
Oh you, you, yeah, you
You, you, love, you
N' you, yes you, love me.

Later on, he coos:

And when
I'm holding you
Ooh, what a feeling
Seems too good to be true
That I'm telling you all
That I must be dreaming.

In the other, "Can't Stop Thinking about You," he repeats the title verse, or something close to it, 28 times, almost two-thirds the whole piece:

And when the nighttime comes
    around
Daylight has left me
I can't take it
If I don't see you no more.

These love ballads are lyrical regressions to earlier Beatle works. Though they indicate the intensity and devotion of a true love, they do so in near-parody, as if Harrison's most sophisticated expressions of love are the most ambiguous ones. When he most needs to express a personal love out of deep *human* need, he does so in a self-mocking and sabotaging juvenile fashion. Perhaps the directness of this kind of relationship causes a conflict absent in a divinely spiritual, impersonal love.

However, ultimately this LP points toward the hopefulness and firmness of Harrison's follow-up to *Extra Texture,* his *Thirty-Three and a Third. Extra Texture*'s "The Answer's at the End," there is a conciliatory tone of sorts, a spiritual detente between Harrison and all the people he's known, loved, wronged, hurt, and been wounded by.

Scan not a friend with a micro-
    scopic glass
You know his faults now let his
    foibles pass

Later, he turns this around with refreshing egalitarianism:

You know my faults now let the
    foibles pass
Life is one long enigma, my friend
Live on, live on, the answer's at the
    end.
Don't be so hard on the ones that
    you love
It's the ones that you love we think
    so little of.

On *Thirty-Three and a Third,* he repeats this all-inclusive fellowship in "See Yourself":

It's easier to tell a lie than it is to tell
    the truth
It's easier to kill a fly than it is to
    turn it loose.
It's easier to criticize somebody
    else
Than to see yourself.

On the "See Yourself" track:

It's easier to hurt someone and
    make them cry
Than it is to dry their eyes.

In "The Answer's at the End," Harrison had sung simply and knowingly:

But what's often in your heart
Is the hardest thing to reach
And life is one long mystery, my
    friend.

The inclusion of the "friend"—Dylan did it in "Blowing in the Wind"—has the effect of re-establishing humility and a sense of shared struggle that pervaded *All Things,* but little of Harri-

son's more subsequent and condescending work until 1976. He has come to terms with himself now, and is more humbly accepting of his and others' weaknesses, flaws, and desires. Perhaps after ten years, with a firmer spiritual ground beneath him, he is feeling less defensive. "It's all up to what you value," he sings on "It's What You Value" on *Thirty-Three and a Third* in 1976:

Down to where you are
It all swings on the pain you've
    gone through
Getting where you are.

In his delightfully lilting "Crackerbox Palace," which becomes a metaphor for all material physical reality, Harrison sings:

While growing up or trying to
Not knowing where to start
I looked around for someone who
May help reveal my heart.

In part the someone he found appears in "Dear One," a song dedicated to the yogi Paramahansa Yogananda:

Dear One show me—simple Grace
Move me toward Thee—with each
    pace.

And yet, in more than any previous LP since *All Things,* Harrison achieves a sublime balance between the spiritual and the mundane. In his marvelous satire of the plagiarism suit, he states:

This song has nothing tricky
    about it
This song ain't black or white and
    as far as I know
Don't infringe on anyone's
    copyright, so. . .

The tune, secular, humorous, vibrating with musical life, was a bit hit single, Harrison's first in several years. It was reassuring. If Harrison was singing "It's what you value," then perhaps the single—and the LP itself—proved that after years of often murky, idiosyncratic creations, he and his millions of fans could now share again this one lasting, precious value: a desire to hear George Harrison—or Hari Georgeson, Jai Hari Sein, L'Angelo Mysterioso, or whoever he wanted to be known as, by any other name, alias, or Krishna cryptogram— make the music that makes people move and brings them that ineffable joy that only a great rock and roll song can bring.

Joseph Sia.

DISCOGRAPHY

Meet The Beatles
(Capitol, January 1964)

I Want to Hold Your Hand
I Saw Her Standing There
This Boy
It Won't Be Long
All I've Got to Do
All My Loving
Don't Bother Me
Little Child
*Till There Was You
Hold Me Tight
I Wanna Be Your Man
Not a Second Time

The Beatles' Second Album
(Capitol, April 1964)

*Roll Over Beethoven
Thank You Girl
*You Really Got a Hold on Me
*Devil in Her Heart
*Money
You Can't Do That
*Long Tall Sally
I Call Your Name
*Please Mister Postman
I'll Get You
She Loves You

A Hard Day's Night
(United Artists, June 1964)

A Hard Day's Night
I Should Have Known Better
If I Fell
I'm Happy Just to Dance with You
And I Love Her
Tell Me Why
Can't Buy Me Love
Any Time at All
I'll Cry Instead
Ringo's Theme (This Boy)

Something New
(Capitol, July 1964)

I'll Cry Instead
Things We Said Today
Any Time at All
When I Get Home

---

* Not a Beatles' song.
† Savage Records in New York City released an album containing eight songs recorded by the Beatles before Ringo Starr was a member of the group. The album was entitled *This Is the Savage Young Beatles*. Only one song, an instrumental entitled "Cry for a Shadow," was a Beatles' composition (Lennon-Harrison), which disproves the theory of those who claim that the song entitled "Flying," an instrumental on *Magical Mystery Tour*, was the Beatles' first instrumental. Originally recorded in Hamburg, Germany, in 1961, the album was not released in the United States until the Beatles had become successful with Ringo in the group.

Slow Down
*Matchbox
Tell Me Why
And I Love Her
I'm Happy Just to Dance with You
If I Fell
Komm Gib Mir Deine Hand

The Beatles' Story—
On Stage with the Beatles
(Capitol, November 1964)

How Beatlemania Began
Beatlemania in Action
Man behind the Beatles—Brian
   Epstein, John Lennon
Who's a Millionaire?
The Beatles Look at Life
"Victims" of Beatlemania
Beatle Medley
Ringo Starr
Liverpool and All the World!
Beatles Will Be Beatles
Man behind the Music—George
   Martin, George Harrison
A Hard Day's Night
Paul McCartney, Sneaky Haircuts

Beatles '65
(Capitol, December 1964)

No Reply
I'm a Loser
Baby's in Black
*Rock and Roll Music
I'll Follow the Sun
*Mr. Moonlight
*Honey Don't
I'll Be Back
She's a Woman
I Feel Fine
*Everybody's Trying to Be My Baby

The Early Beatles
(Capitol, March 1965)

Love Me Do
*Twist and Shout
*Anna
*Chains
*Boys
Ask Me Why
Please Please Me
PS I Love You
*Baby It's You
*A Taste of Honey
Do You Want to Know a Secret

Beatles VI
(Capitol, June 1965)

Kansas City
Eight Days a Week
You Like Me Too Much
Bad Boy

Beatles' albums released in U.S.†

Retna.
Early Beatles
BBC TV show,
1964

Dr. Robert
Yesterday
*Act Naturally
And Your Bird Can Sing
If I Needed Someone
We Can Work It Out
What Goes On
Day Tripper

Revolver
(*Capitol, August 1966*)

Taxman (*Harrison*)
Eleanor Rigby
Love You Too (Harrison)
Here, There and Everywhere
Yellow Submarine
She Said She Said
Good Day Sunshine
For No One
I Want to Tell You (*Harrison*)
Got to Get You into My Life
Tomorrow Never Knows

Sgt. Pepper's Lonely Hearts Club Band
(*Capitol, June 1967*)

Sgt. Pepper's Lonely Hearts
  Club Band
A Little Help from My Friends
Lucy in the Sky with Diamonds
Getting Better
Fixing a Hole
She's Leaving Home
Being for the Benefit of Mr. Kite
Within You Without You (*Harrison*)
When I'm Sixty-four
Lovely Rita
Good Morning, Good Morning
Sgt. Pepper's Lonely Hearts
  Club Band (reprise)
A Day in the Life

Magical Mystery Tour
(*Capitol, November 1967*)

Magical Mystery Tour
The Fool on the Hill
Flying (*Lennon, McCartney, Harrison, Starr*)
Blue Jay Way (*Harrison*)
Your Mother Should Know
I Am the Walrus
Hello Goodbye
Strawberry Fields Forever
Penny Lane
Baby, You're a Rich Man
All You Need Is Love

---

†Although this album was issued after *Rubber Soul*, it is a collection of early singles issued in the United States and in England that were all recorded before *Rubber Soul*.

I Don't Want to Spoil the Party
Words of Love
What You're Doing
Yes It Is
*Dizzy Miss Lizzie
Tell Me What You See
Every Little Thing

Help!
(*Capitol, August 1965*)

Help!
The Night Before
From Me to You Fantasy
You've Got to Hide Your Love Away
I Need You (*Harrison*)
In the Tyrol
Another Girl
Another Hard Day's Night
Ticket to Ride
The Bitter End
You Can't Do That
You're Going to Lose That Girl
The Chase

Rubber Soul
(*Capitol, December 1965*)

I've Just Seen a Face
Norwegian Wood
You Won't See Me
Think for Yourself (*Harrison*)
The Word
Michelle
It's Only Love
Girl
I'm Looking Through You
In My Life
Wait
Run for Your Life

"Yesterday"... and Today
(*Capitol, June 1966*)†

Drive My Car
I'm Only Sleeping
Nowhere Man

Yellow Submarine
SW 153, 1968

Yellow Submarine
Only a Northern Song - Harrison
All Together Now
Hey Bulldog
It's All Too Much (*Harrison*)
All You Need Is Love
Pepperland
Sea of Time & Sea of Holes
Sea of Monsters
March of the Meanies
Pepperland Laid Waste
Yellow Submarine in Pepperland

The Beatles
SKBO 3404, 1968

Back in the USSR
Dear Prudence
Glass Onion
Ob-la-di, Ob-la-da
Wild Honey Pie
The Continuing Story of Bungalo Bill
While My Guitar Gently Weeps
    (*Harrison*)
Happiness Is a Warm Gun
Martha My Dear
I'm So Tired
Blackbird
Piggies (*Harrison*)
Rocky Raccoon
Don't Pass Me By
Why Don't We Do It in the Road?
I Will
Julia
Birthday
Yer Blues
Mother Nature's Son
Everybody's Got Something to Hide
    Except Me and My Monkey
Sexy Sadie
Helter Skelter
Long Long Long (*Harrison*)
Revolution 1
Honey Pie
Savoy Truffle (*Harrison*)
Cry Baby Cry
Revolution 9
Goodnight

Abbey Road
SO-383, 1969

Come Together
Something (*Harrison*)
Maxwell's Silver Hammer
Oh! Darling
Octopus's Garden
I Want You (She's So Heavy)
Here Comes the Sun (*Harrison*)
Because
You Never Give Me Your Money
Sun King

Mean Mr. Mustard
Polythene Pam
She Came In Through the Bathroom
    Window
Golden Slumbers
Carry That Weight
The End

Hey Jude
Cap 385, 1970

Hey Jude
Revolution
Paperback Writer
I Should Have Known Better
Lady Madonna
Can't Buy Me Love
Don't Let Me Down
Ballad of John and Yoko
Rain
Old Brown Shoe (*Harrison*)

Let It Be
Apple 34001, 1970

Two Of Us
I Dig a Pony
Across The Universe
I Me Mine (*Harrison*)
Dig It
Let It Be
Maggie Mae
I've Got a Feeling
One After 909
The Long and Winding Road
For You Blue (*Harrison*)
Get Back

Rex Features.
With Jackie Lomax

Beatles' single records released in U.S.

Please Please Me / Ask Me Why (*VJ, 1963-64*)
From Me to You / Thank You Girl (*VJ, 1963-64*)
Do You Want to Know a Secret (*VJ, 1963-64*)
*Twist and Shout (*VJ, 1963-64*)
Love Me Do / PS I Love You (*VJ, 1963-64*)
She Loves You / I'll Get You (*Swan, August 1963*)
I Want to Hold Your Hand / I Saw Her Standing There
　　(*Capitol, January 1964*)
Can't Buy Me Love / You Can't Do That (*Capitol, March 1964*)
Sie Liebt Dich (*Swan, May 1964*)
A Hard Day's Night / I Should Have Known Better (*Capitol,
　　July 1964*)
I'll Cry Instead / I'm Happy Just to Dance with You
　　(*Capitol, July 1964*)
And I Love Her / If I Fell (*Capitol, July 1964*)
*Slow Down / Matchbox (*Capitol, August 1964*)
I Feel Fine / She's a Woman (*Capitol, November 1964*)
By the Beatles (*Capitol EP, February 1965*);
　　*Honey Don't / I'm a Loser / *Mr. Moonlight /
　　*Everybody's Trying to Be My Baby
Eight Days a Week / I Don't Want to Spoil the Party
　　(*Capitol, February 1965*)
Ticket to Ride / Yes It Is (*Capitol, April 1965*)
Help! / I'm Down (*Capitol, July 1965*)
*Act Naturally / Yesterday (*Capitol, September 1965*)
We Can Work It Out / Day Tripper (*Capitol, December
　　1965*)
Nowhere Man / What Goes On (*Capitol, February 1966*)
Paperback Writer / Rain (*Capitol, May 1966*)
Yellow Submarine / Eleanor Rigby (*Capitol, August 1966*)
Strawberry Fields Forever / Penny Lane (*Capitol, February
　　1967*)
Baby, You're a Rich Man / All You Need Is Love (*Capitol, July 1967*)
Hello Goodbye / I Am the Walrus (*Capitol, November 1967*)
Lady Madonna / The Inner Light (*Capitol, March 1968*)
Revolution / Hey Jude (*Apple, August 1968*)

Wonderwall Music
ST 3350, 1968

Microbes
Red Lady Too
Tabla and Pakavaj
In The Park
Drilling a Home
Guru Vandana
Greasy Legs
Ski-ing and Gat Kirwani
Dream Scene
Party Seacombe
Love Scene
Crying
Cowboy Museum
Fantasy Sequins
Glass Box
On The Bed
Wonderwall to Be Here
Singing Om

Electronic Sounds
Apple 3358, 1969

Under the Mersey Wall
No Time or Space

All Things Must Pass
Apple STCH 639, 1970

My Sweet Lord
Isn't It A Pity
All Things Must Pass
I'd Have You Anytime
Wah-Wah
What Is Life
If Not For You
Behind That Locked Door
Let It Down
Run Of The Mill
Beware of Darkness
Apple Scruffs
Ballad of Sir Frankie Crisp (Let It
   Roll)
Awaiting On You All
Art of Dying
I Dig Love
Hear Me Lord
Out Of The Blue
Plug Me In
I Remember Jeep
Thanks For The Pepperoni

The Concert for Bangla-Desh
Apple 3385, 1972

Ravi Shankar, Ali Akbar Khan, Alla
   Rakah:
   Bangla Dhun
George Harrison:
   Wah-Wah
   My Sweet Lord
   Here Comes The Sun
   Awaiting On You All

Bangla Desh
Something
Billy Preston:
   That's The Way God Planned It
Ringo Starr:
   It Don't Come Easy
George Harrison, Leon Russell:
   Beware Of Darkness
George Harrison, Eric Clapton:
   While My Guitar Gently Weeps
Leon Russell, Don Preston:
   Jumpin' Jack Flash
   Youngblood
Bob Dylan:
   Hard Rain's Gonna Fall
   It Takes A Lot To Laugh, It Takes A
      Train To Cry
   Blowin' In The Wind
   Mr. Tambourine Man
   Just Like A Woman

Living In The Material World
Apple SMAS 3410, 1973

Living In The Material World
Give Me Love
Sue Me, Sue You Blues
Light That Has Lighted The World
Don't Let Me Wait Too Long
Who Can See It
Lord Loves The One
Be Here Now
Try Some Buy Some
Day The World Gets Round
That Is All

Dark Horse
Apple SMAS 3418, 1974

Hari's On Tour
Simply Shady
So Sad
Bye Bye, Love
Maya Love
Ding Dong, Ding Dong
Dark Horse
Far East Man
It Is "He" (Jai Sri Krishna)

Extra Texture—Read All About It
Apple SW 3420, 1975

You
Answer's At The End
This Guitar (Can't Keep From
   Crying)
Ooh Baby (You Know That I Love
   You)
World Of Stone
Bit More Of You
His Name Is Legs (Ladies &
   Gentlemen)
Can't Stop Thinking About You
Tired of Midnight Blue
Grey Cloudy Lies

Solo Albums:

The Best of George Harrison
ST 11578, 1976

Something (*Abbey Road*)
If I Needed Someone (*Rubber Soul*)
Here Comes The Sun (*Abbey Road*)
Taxman (*Revolver*)
Think For Yourself (*Rubber Soul*)
For You Blue (*Let It Be*)
While My Guitar Gently Weeps (*The Beatles*)
My Sweet Lord (*All Things Must Pass*)
Give Me Love (*Living In The Material World*)
You (*Extra Texture*)
Bangla-desh (*Concert For Bangla-desh*)
Dark Horse (*Dark Horse*)
What Is Life (*All Things Must Pass*)

33⅓
DKH 3005, 1976

Woman Don't You Cry For Me
Dear One
Beautiful Girl
This Song
See Yourself
It's What You Value
True Love
Pure Smokey
Crackerbox Palace
Learning How To Love You

Solo Singles:

Apple Scruffs (*Cap 1828*)
Bangla-desh (*Cap 1836*)
Crackerbox Palace (*DKH 8313*)
Dark Horse (*Cap 6245*)
Deep Blue (*Cap 1836*)
Ding Dong, Ding Dong (*Cap 1879*)
Give Me Love (*Cap 1862*)
Hari's On Tour (*Cap 1862*)
Isn't It A Pity (*Cap 2995*)

Learning How To Love You (*DKH 8294, 8313*)
Maya Love (*Cap 1885*)
Miss O'Dell (*Cap 1862*)
My Sweet Lord (*Cap 2995*)
This Guitar (*Cap 1885*)
This Song (*DKH 8294*)
What Is Life (*Cap 1828*)
You (*Cap 6245*)

Retna.
George at home